A Minister's Manual
for Spiritual Warfare

A Minister's Manual
for Spiritual Warfare

Mark Allen Quay

Foreword by
Archbishop Foley Beach

RESOURCE *Publications* · Eugene, Oregon

Resource Publications
An Imprint of Wipf and Stock Publishers
199 W. 8th Ave., Suite 3
Eugene, OR 97401

www.wipfandstock.com

ISBN 13: 978-1-4982-3853-3

Manufactured in the U.S.A.   11/25/2015

"There are things that go bump in the night . . . make no mistake. And we are the ones who bump back."[1]

To all the ministers "who bump back"—there will be a jewel in your crown.

---

1. Line spoken by the character Trevor "Broom" Bruttenholm played by John Hurt in the movie *Hellboy*.

An Invocation

In the name of God, the Father, the Son, and the Holy Spirit! Amen.

May the power of Almighty God, the Father, the Son, and the Holy Spirit equip you for every good work, doing that which is well pleasing in His sight. Amen.

May He give you His strength and the power of His might to resist the enemy and put him to flight. Amen.

May He give you wisdom and discernment to know and understand the attacks of the wicked one. Amen.

May He surround you and guard you with the presence of his Spirit and the armies of heaven: the Cherubim and Seraphim, the Powers and Virtues, the Archangels, the Guardians, and all the angelic hosts. Amen.

May He cause you, by His grace and power, to be a warrior in the very image of Jesus the Messiah, the Son of the Virgin Mary, and give you strength to crush the head of that old serpent, the devil, beneath your feet. Amen, alleluia!

Contents

List of Illustrations

All figures by Grace Wiley. Used by permission.

Foreword

A BOOK ON SPIRITUAL warfare? A manual for training ministers to deliver human beings from evil spirits? A person might think I had lost my mind for writing a foreword for such a book! No, I am not mad, I am just following the teaching of the New Testament and the historical tradition of the church.

In the New Testament it is clear there are dimensions of reality which are beyond flesh and blood. It is the spiritual realm, and it is quite active. In the ministry of Jesus we see him dealing with demons and evil spirits again and again (see Matt 8:28-34; 9:32-34; 17:14-21). If Jesus had to deliver people from the oppression of the evil one and his demons, it should not surprise us that his ministers will be called to the ministry of deliverance as well.

Jesus knew his followers would face this reality in their ministries. In the name of Jesus Christ, through his blood shed on the cross, and by the power of the Holy Spirit, followers of Jesus have what is necessary to overcome any attack of the evil one (see Luke 10:17-20). The problem we modern-day ministers have is our lack of knowledge and training in spiritual warfare.

The Apostle Paul wrote to the Christians in Ephesus to stand firm in their faith and not be overcome by the evil one. In Ephesians 6:10-18 he shares how to do this.

First, "Be strong in God and his mighty power" (10). As followers of Jesus, we have access to the authority of God through the presence and power of the Holy Spirit. As we learn to abide in

Jesus Christ (John 15:5) and yield to the Holy Spirit's leading in our lives, we become spiritually strong. God's power is stronger than any power on earth or in the spiritual realm.

Second, the Apostle writes to "put on the full armor of God" (11). Why? So that the follower of Jesus can stand against the devil's schemes and devices. The Apostle Peter writes, "Your enemy the devil prowls around like a roaring lion looking for someone to devour. Resist him, standing firm in the faith . . ." (1 Pet 5:8-9, *NIV*). The devil is a deceiver (Rev 12:9), who, Jesus says, "seeks to kill, steal, and destroy" (John 10:10). Living and ministering within the protection of the full armor of God (Jesus) is crucial in spiritual warfare.

Third, Paul encourages the believer to "put on Jesus" using the "full armor of God" (11). Each illustration from the Roman soldier's battle uniform is an attribute of Jesus. Notice that Paul very clearly says who the enemy is not (12)—our brother or sister in Christ! When sincere followers of Jesus are arguing with one another and fighting among themselves, the enemy is rejoicing. The focus is off the real enemy and we become spiritually unfit to join in the fight. Our battle is with rulers, authorities, powers of this dark world, and spiritual forces of evil in the heavenly realms (12). Standing firm and taking authority over the power of demonic activity is where the battle is fought and won. When followers of Jesus are attacked, Paul wants them to be able to stand firm! Four times in Ephesians 6 he exhorts followers of Jesus to "stand"!

Last, but far from least, the Apostle reminds his readers of the importance of prayer (18). In dealing with the evil one, prayer (and often fasting) is crucial for unleashing the power of God. Not only should prayer be a part of any deliverance ministry, but intercessors (prayer warriors) should be lifting up all the people involved on the ministry team in immediate and specific prayer. Nothing is accomplished without prayer, and this is especially true in the spiritual realm. Pray! Pray! Pray!

Like people of Paul's time, we find ourselves in a period in which demonic activity is becoming more obvious in the public square, in our congregations, and even among Christians. It is not that the enemy has more power; rather, the spiritual covering over our land is being lifted because of our nation's disobedience and rebellion against God and his Law.

Every Christian, and especially ministers of the Gospel, must be knowledgeable and open to the gifts of the Holy Spirit and learn how to use them effectively in order to tear down spiritual strongholds, powers, and principalities. Ministers of the Gospel need a clear and orderly understanding of spiritual warfare. Father Mark Quay's *A Minister's Manual for Spiritual Warfare* explains this in detail. It is insightful, balanced, and practical. It will help the minister of the Gospel walk in the power and authority of Jesus.

A Minister's Manual for Spiritual Warfare is just that—a manual. It is a hands-on guidebook for equipping the minister with the knowledge and the skills needed to thwart the schemes of the evil one. Quay does an excellent job of teaching the basics from the Scriptures, using the tradition of the church, while weaving in an understanding from psychology and psychiatry. Written in age of extreme skepticism about spiritual things (even in parts of the church), Quay informs and guides without going off the deep-end into some never-never land of weird spiritualism.

Am I suggesting looking for a demon under every rock? No! But what do you do when you encounter one? How do you genuinely help someone in spiritual bondage? *A Minister's Manual for Spiritual Warfare* will give you the tools.

Through the years as a pastor, there is a verse that often haunts me. In Matthew 17, a man brings his son to Jesus to be delivered and healed from a spirit. He says to Jesus: "I brought him to your disciples and they could not heal him" (Matt 17:16). May God deliver us from evil, and let it be said of this generation, "They laid hands upon the sick and they were healed."

The Most Rev Foley Beach, DMin

Primate and Archbishop, Anglican Church in North America
Bishop Ordinary, Anglican Diocese of the South

Preface

LET ME START BY saying what this small book is not. It is not a scholarly treatise on the nature of evil, demonology, or the psychology of the supernatural. For these subjects I recommend Merrill F. Unger (*Biblical Demonology*), Kurt E. Koch (*Demonology Past and Present*), and T. Craig Isaacs (*Revelations and Possession*). It is not a discussion on the health of the soul and the impact of the demonic thereon. For this, consult Leanne Payne (*The Healing Presence* and *Restoring the Christian Soul*) and Neal Lozano (*Resisting the Devil* and *Unbound*). Nor is it a thoughtful work on spiritual warfare written by a good scholar for the broader public: Michael Harper (*Spiritual Warfare*), Francis McNutt (*Deliverance from Evil Spirits*), and Michael Scanlan (*Deliverance from Evil Spirits,* a different book with the same title) stand out in my mind. Finally it is not a sensational or titillating work, though I have read some of these with much benefit: Gabriele Amorth (*An Exorcist Tells His Stories* and *An Exorcist: More Stories*), Matt Baglio (*The Rite*), and (with some trepidation) Malachi Martin (*Hostage to the Devil*). I also commend John Richards' small book *Exorcism, Deliverance and Healing: Some Pastoral Guidelines.* This book, the results of the Bishop of Exeter's Study Group on Exorcism, is enormously helpful in developing diocesan policies and procedures regarding deliverance ministry.

With the exception of Unger and Koch, all the writers cited above as being in some way authoritative are either Roman

Catholics or Anglicans (though the Anglican priest Michael Harper would later become Eastern Orthodox). This is for a number of reasons about which I will not go into detail. Suffice it to say that scholarly training and biblical accountability are critical for correctly dealing with such a sensitive topic as spiritual warfare.

Instead, this book is a how-to manual—technical, pedestrian, and (I hope) boring. It is not my intention that this book finds its way into the hands of the merely curious or the ill-prepared "week-end warrior" who would very likely do far more damage than good. This is a manual designed primarily for Anglican priests to assist them in the pastoral offices of spiritual warfare. Christian ministers of other traditions will find its contents helpful, as may trained and authorized laymen and women who have a special anointing of the Holy Spirit for this sort of work. It is what the title says, a manual: practical, to-the-point, and (hopefully) useful.

Spiritual warfare is not a war fought in the flesh (Eph 6:12), but in the spiritual realm, which is populated by two kingdoms: Light and Darkness. In considering these principalities, it is important that the Christian warrior understands that he fights not in a battle between two equally opposed armies, but rather in a conflict between the forces of the rightful King, Jesus the Messiah, who has already won the decisive victory through the cross and resurrection, and the defeated, rebellious forces of the evil one, the devil, Satan, the Serpent, that old deceiver and enemy of God and humanity. Have confidence soldier of Christ—your General has triumphed and He invites you to join him beneath his banner.

Warfare requires discipline. It requires training. It requires knowledge of tactics, strategy, and the overall battle plan of the commanding general. Throughout the history of the people of God—both Israel and the church—worship in Word, Prayer, and Sacrament has been used as the devastating weapon *par excellence* against the regiments of the wicked. This weapon is, in a word, liturgy.

Some readers may ask, "Why do we need liturgy in spiritual warfare when praying in the name of Jesus without the use of ritual should be just as, if not more, effective?" No doubt there are spiritual warriors who do have such a powerful anointing that, at their mere mention of the name of Jesus, the enemy retreats. I have met such people. It also should be the case that all ministers, be they lay or ordained, have the spiritual gifts and anointing necessary for this warfare, at least to some extent.

Yet, it is too often true that a lot of mistakes are made and much damage is done by sincere believers, many of whom do have a genuine calling to this ministry. It is my experience (and that of several others far more experienced than I) that the spiritual atmosphere of a deliverance session, especially during an exorcism, can be so confusing that the priest or minister may be at a loss for words.

Additionally, there are many aspects of spiritual warfare that the collected wisdom of the church has found to be important, and it is difficult for the priest or minister to remember them all. Remember, the church has been engaged in this warfare since its inception, and the church Fathers have much to teach us. Therefore, the liturgy, if it is biblical, is of great value—it is the expression of the Lord's tactics, strategy, and battle plan set into magnificent prose, using the words or ideas of the Holy Scriptures and the sacred orthodox teachings given to the church by the Spirit of the living God.

However—and this is important—the liturgies of spiritual warfare are never a substitute for a genuine anointing of the Holy Spirit for this work. Nor is an anointed gifting for warfare a substitute for following the tactics laid out by Scripture and the godly, orthodox traditions of the church. In 2 Timothy 3:5, we read "Having a form of godliness, but denying the power thereof" (KJV).[1] The word "form" is *morphōsis* in the Greek, which means form, structure, or appropriate appearance.[2] One could paraphrase this as "They have the right form, but they don't have the power to minister appropriately." I have sometimes likened this to the minister being a locomotive, the form being the tracks, and the power

---

1. The use here of the KJV notwithstanding, unless otherwise indicated, scripture quotations throughout this work are from The Holy Bible, English Standard Version (Carol Stream: Crossway, 2001). Used by permission.

2. It can also mean "mere appearance," but that does not change my point.

being a head of steam. If there is no steam, the locomotive goes
nowhere. If there are no tracks, the locomotive careens around the
countryside, leaving devastation in its wake. The locomotive must
have both power and form. Neither is sufficient in themselves.
Both are necessary.

These prayers and rites which follow are derived from the
various sources noted, appropriately modified where necessary
to be in conformity with the teachings of the Anglican doctrinal
norms (i.e., chiefly the Bible, as well as The Thirty-nine Articles
of Religion and The Book of Common Prayer and its Ordinal).
They are not the only means of battle. There are other forms. Also,
one must not neglect the ordinary but powerful weapons of daily
prayer, reading from the Scriptures, worship in Word and Sacrament, and holiness of life. It is my prayer that this manual will
assist many in the ongoing work of spiritual warfare with greater
boldness and authority.

Onward, Christian soldier. Soldier of Christ, arise!

The Rev. Mark A. Quay, DMinEd, DMin

Rector, St. Peter's Anglican Church
Birmingham, Alabama
Formerly President and Dean
Anglican School of Ministry
Little Rock, Arkansas

Acknowledgments

I WISH I COULD acknowledge the contributions of everyone over the years that helped me either in writing this manual or in gaining the experience and training I needed. But, since I can't remember them all, here are those I can. With the exception of my wife and son, they are listed in no particular order.

Jani Quay, my wife: for many years of support for this work in particular.

Noah Quay, my son: who provided me with some of my best sources.

Grace Wiley, my daughter: she did the extensive and tedious work of checking tenses, number agreement, voice consistency, and a host of other corrections. Thanks to her as well for her simple, elegant drawings.

The Rev Job Serebrov, JD, LLM, of Little Rock, Arkansas, an Anglican priest with the Convocation of Anglicans in North America and former canon lawyer with the Anglican Church in America: my legal eagle.

Mari Serebrov, writer and contributing editor at Thomson Reuters, Essex, Vermont: for understanding how informed consent, liability, and public relations disasters work.

The Rev T. Craig Isaacs, PhD, clinical psychologist in private practice and Anglican priest, San Rafael, California;

ACKNOWLEDGMENTS

Richard Shelton, MD, Charles B. Ireland Professor and Vice Chair for Research, Department of Psychiatry, School of Medicine, University of Alabama at Birmingham; and

Kenneth M. Stoltzfus, PhD, Associate Professor and Chair, Department of Social Work, School of Public Health, Samford University, Birmingham, Alabama: for clinical insight from a greatly appreciated biblical perspective.

The Very Rev Henry Baldwin, PhD, Dean of Holy Cross Cathedral, Loganville, Georgia; former Dean and Associate Professor of Biblical Studies, Anglican School of Ministry, Little Rock, Arkansas (now merged with Trinity School for Ministry, Ambridge, Pennsylvania);

The Rev Lyle Dorsett, PhD, Billy Graham Professor of Evangelism, Beeson Divinity School, Birmingham, Alabama, and Rector of Christ the King Anglican Church; and

The Rev Michael Pahls, PhD, former Assistant Professor of Theological Studies, Anglican School of Ministry, and currently Adjunct Instructor in Theology at both Christian Brothers College and Memphis Theological Seminary, Memphis, Tennessee: for well-grounded pastoral, biblical, and theological advice (and corrections).

Marjean Brooks, Christian writer and editor, Birmingham, Alabama: editor extraordinaire and assassin of all things ungrammatical or stylistically awkward (any problems in grammar or style are the result of my intransigence). I'm also grateful for the use of her and her husband Ricky's lake house as a getaway to work on this book.

Lynette McCary, the "little old lady" from Birmingham, Alabama, who defies all little old lady conventions: her cabin in Mentone, Alabama provided me with sanctuary to write much of this manual in peace.

The Rev Herb Hand, DMin, Rector, Faith Anglican Church, Cordova, Tennessee: for encouragement during a particularly rough patch and the opportunity to try out some of this material on his unsuspecting congregation.

The Most Rev Foley Beach, DMin, Primate and Archbishop, Anglican Church in North America, my Ordinary and father in Christ: for his loving and much needed kick-in-the-pants for me to get the work done.

The Most Rev Emmanuel Kolini, former Primate and Archbishop, Province of the Anglican Church of Rwanda: he helped me see what was at stake.

The Rt Rev Derek Jones, Bishop of the Special Jurisdiction of the Armed Forces and Chaplaincy, Anglican Church in North America: for encouragement and helping me see the need.

To all, both remembered and unremembered, my most heart-felt thanks.

Abbreviations

ACLS: Advanced Cardiac Life Support.

ATLS: Advance Trauma Life Support.

SOAP: Subjective Component, Objective Component, Assessment, and Plan.

1

Demonic Attacks: How to Identify and Diagnose Them

Introduction

A PARISHIONER WALKS INTO your office and tells you of his struggles. After completing his story, he wonders aloud, "Am I under some kind of spiritual attack?" How do you move forward?

Identifying and diagnosing the nature of a demonic attack is often difficult. It may be challenging to distinguish between someone suffering from the consequences of a persistent sin as opposed to someone who is demonically oppressed. It requires wisdom, prayer, discernment, and conversation with everyone involved: the victim, his family and friends, and members of your discernment team (more on the latter later on). It may also require consultation with medical and mental health professionals to identify any underlying physical or mental health issues.

Before continuing, a word of admonition: do not engage in spiritual warfare unless you are confident that there will be follow-through by the victim, which includes participation in the life of a church, regular partaking of the sacraments, and daily Christian disciplines (e.g., prayer, Scripture reading, and so forth).

When determining the nature of a demonic attack, be aware that a common misconception is that demonic attacks are *always* the result of sin in the life of the one attacked. Certainly, there is a correlation between persistent, sinful behavior and demonic attack. Yet it is not unusual for seemingly innocent people to become victims of the forces of evil for no apparent reason or because of the sins of others (the latter is especially true in the case of curses).

An important thought before you read further: prayer is a constant necessity. You may think it goes without saying, but it does not. It is too easy to get involved in doing ministry without first resorting to the company of God through prayer, especially listening prayer. Begin every session of deliverance ministry, including training, with prayer. Take prayer breaks throughout. End with prayer. Whatever else you may do, pray.

Some Definitions

The minister: an ordained and appropriately trained minister of the Gospel authorized by the proper Church authorities to conduct the pastoral offices connected with spiritual warfare. It may also include suitably authorized and trained laymen and women as well.

The victim: a person undergoing a demonic attack. The victim may be a willing participant in the deliverance or an unwilling and uncooperative person.

Deliverance ministry: any action by a Christian, done in the name of Jesus, which seeks to remove or lessen the spiritual bondage which comes with undergoing a demonic attack. This especially applies to the ministry of church-authorized ministers.

Mental Health

Obviously, the issue of mental health comes up in the subject of spiritual warfare—is what is being observed a mental health condition, or is it a true spiritual attack? This may in fact be a false dichotomy. Some instances are purely a matter of a personality disorder, anxiety disorder, or psychosis. However, it is seldom the case that people under spiritual attack do not display mental problems, if for no other reason than because they are exhausted and depressed by the constant onslaught. Mental health problems may cause a weakness of the will or constitution that can lead to spiritual attack and, conversely, spiritual attack can lead to mental health problems. The Rev Dr T. Craig Isaacs provides a helpful suggestion: mental conditions often have the sense of arising from within the victim, while conditions of a spiritual origin seem to arise from without.[1]

It is important therefore to involve mental health practitioners, especially a clinical psychologist or a psychiatrist, as much as possible. Understand that it may be difficult to find such a practitioner who will be sympathetic to the spiritual warfare ministry, let alone one who understands the spiritual dynamics involved. Even Christian professionals, many of whom are trained at secular institutions, may hesitate to be involved, fearing the potential negative impact on their careers.

1. Isaacs, *Revelations and Possession*, 79-88.

If the mental health professional determines treatment is needed, either before deliverance or concurrent with it, understand that it may take time for the treatment to have its desired effects. This will require coordination with a therapist, which in turn may require written authorization from the victim for the two of you to exchange information.

Medical Conditions

An additional consideration is the matter of underlying physical health issues. A large variety of medical conditions can cause behavioral disorders that may appear to be spiritual in origin. Untreated diabetes, neurological diseases, disorders of the thyroid, and a host of other illnesses can make distinguishing between what is of the natural world and of the supernatural word extremely difficult. I personally know of someone whose migraines led to such bizarre behavior as rages, hallucinations, and jumbled and disjointed speech. In my earlier, spiritually naïve days, I would certainly have been tempted to ascribe a demonic origin to this. Just as it is necessary to get the cooperation of a mental health provider, so it is with a medical practitioner (preferably an internist or family practitioner).

The minister should keep in mind that deliverance, especially exorcism, is physically, emotionally, and mentally taxing.[2] It is necessary for the minister to determine if there are any sort of health factors concerning him, his team, and the victim that need to be taken into consideration before beginning any deliverance ministry.

I recommend that during a difficult deliverance session,[3] especially an exorcism, the presence of a medically qualified person with ACLS training (the additional qualification of ATLS training would be even better). Paramedics, emergency room nurses, and physicians are good examples of such. The minister should pay serious attention to this person's recommendations, including taking

2. Anytime a deliverance session becomes too difficult for the minister or the victim, it can be stopped and resumed later.

3. Again, please keep in mind you can always halt a session if needed.

a rest break. This would allow the victim to physically recover, or the medical personnel to put the deliverance session on hold until a medical assessment can be made.

A final note on both medical and mental health aspects and demonization: often the people who come to you or are referred for deliverance have already seen a number of professionals and found, despite the best efforts modern medical or mental health sciences can offer, they have not improved. This can provide an important diagnostic consideration.[4]

Types of Attacks

There are a lot of opinions regarding the types of demonic attack. The New Testament has two different ways to describe those under attack: "to have a demon" (*echō daimonion)* and "to be demonized" (*daimonizomai)*. Perhaps a better way to understand demonic activity would be to describe it as a continuum, much like autism has come to be understood. However, for the sake of utility, let us say there are five types of demonic attacks: oppression, obsession, possession, haunting, and curses. It is possible, even likely, that more two or more of these may occur simultaneously.

Diagnosis

It is especially important in a difficult situation, such as when the victim's problems are chronic or severe, to get an accurate diagnosis of his/her condition. Diagnostic questions and considerations are given below for each type of attack. Remember that different kinds of attacks may occur simultaneously.

A side note: while what follows has an almost clinical approach, in dealing with demons you are not engaging in a scientific diagnosis and treatment of a pathology. Demons are persons, not bacteria or viruses, and they will use their intelligence and experience to fight against you. This is spiritual warfare, after all.

4. Amorth, *An Exorcist Tells His Story,* 91-92.

In difficult cases, the minister would do well to keep accurate records. One way to do so is to follow the SOAP process.[5] An example of an actual use of SOAP can be found in appendix A.

Subjective Component: record the victim's history. Include self-reports and those of family and friends when possible.

Objective Component: record your personal observations of the victim's behavior including responses to prayer, answers to questions, body language, and peculiarities of speech (verbal expressions and tone). Also include observations from trusted and trained ministers and laymen/women, and from medical and mental health professionals.

Assessment: write your conclusions based up the above components. Include mental health, physical health, and spiritual health assessments. Remember, if you are not a medical or mental health professional, you should not make medical or mental health diagnoses.

Plan: develop a plan for deliverance ministry. You should include the following: additional assessment needed, victim self-care, program for deliverance, ministry team composition, and victim post-deliverance self-care.

General Diagnostic Questions

The following questions should be asked of all who present themselves for deliverance. It would be helpful to get others who know this person to answer them as well.

---

5. I am not suggesting that the seemingly objective, scientific approach given here is the only approach to structure deliverance ministry, nor do I suggest that demonization is to be handled like any medical condition. Instead, I am recommending this method as one way to approach accountability and record keeping.

1. Are you a Christian? Do you trust in Jesus Christ as your only Lord and Savior? Tell me about your relationship with the Lord.

2. Are you a member of a church? Which one? How often do you attend? In what activities are you involved?

3. Have you been baptized? When was the last time you received Holy Communion?

4. Tell me what it was like for you growing up.

5. Are you married? Do you have children? Tell me about your family.

6. Describe your life now. What about it makes you happy? Sad?

7. Tell me about your physical health. Mental. Emotional. Spiritual.

8. Do you have any areas in your life of persistent struggle with sin? Tell me about them.

9. Do you believe you are under spiritual attack? Has someone told you are under such an attack? How have you responded to this?

Oppression

Oppression is a demonic attack that lowers the wellbeing—the physical, mental, emotional, and spiritual constitution—of the victim. It can take the form of ill health, depression, suicidal thoughts, a sense of hopelessness or pessimism, lassitude, or powerlessness. The following questions should be asked by the minister to explore the possibility of a diagnosis of oppression.

Diagnostic Questions

1. Illnesses

    a. Do you have any unexplained illnesses?

    b. Do you suffer from illnesses that tend to run in your family?

    c. Have you seen a physician about them? If so, what did he/she say?

    d. Are you being faithful to the assigned course of treatment?

2. Sadness/Depression

    a. Are you sad? Are you a normally sad person?

    b. Is there a reason for this sadness, for example, the loss of a job, death of a family member, or marital problems?

    c. Would you say that you are depressed, "feeling blue," or lacking in energy more than usual?

    d. Do you find it difficult to perform tasks that were once easy? Do you have problems sleeping?

    e. Have you seen a physician or mental health provider about this? If so, what did he/she say?

    f. Are you being faithful to the assigned course of treatment?

3. Suicide

    a. Do you think about harming or killing yourself?

    b. If so, how would you do it?

    c. Are these thoughts continuous or only occasional?

    d. Do you have a reason why you are thinking these thoughts, for example a family or work problem for which there seems to be no solution?

    e. Have you seen a mental health practitioner about this? If so, what did he/she say?

    f. Are you being faithful to the assigned course of treatment?

4. Disquiet

    a. Are you experiencing anything else that affects your sense of well-being, such as a sense of unease, "impending doom," or "waiting for the other shoe to drop?"

    b. How would you describe it?

    c. Have you sought help about this?

Obsession

Obsession could probably be treated as a form of oppression, but it is so prevalent in Western society, it deserves separate consideration. Obsession is an attack in that the victim's thoughts and actions are unnaturally focused on an idea, person, object, or behavior, perhaps nearly to the exclusion of all other things. Sexual thoughts, compulsive destructive behaviors, or addictions *may* be symptoms of this.

Diagnostic Questions

1. People Obsessions

   a. Do you find yourself constantly thinking about a person?

   b. Is there a reason for this, for example, a person in your family who is in trouble or a person to whom you find you are sexually attracted?

   c. Would you say you think too much about this person?

   d. Do you find yourself distracted from doing normal or necessary life tasks?

   e. Have you interacted with this person in anyway concerning your thoughts toward them?

   f. Have you seen a mental health practitioner about this? If so, what did he/she say?

   g. Are you being faithful to the assigned course of treatment?

2. Material Obsessions

   a. Do you find yourself constantly thinking about an object?

    b. Is there a reason for this, for example, was this something stolen from you or something that has a special significance for you?

    c. Would you say you think too much about this object?

    d. Do you find yourself distracted from doing normal or necessary life tasks?

    e. Have you sought to gain control over this object in a way you have not previously done?

    f. Have you seen a mental health practitioner about this? If so, what did he/she say?

    g. Are you being faithful to the assigned course of treatment?

3. Behavioral Disorders

    a. Do you find yourself behaving in a way that is unusual for you?

    b. Are you doing things you haven't done before?

    c. Would you describe this behavior as negative, destructive, or distracting?

    d. Have others expressed concern about this behavior?

    e. Have you seen a mental health provider about this? If so, what did he/she say?

    f. Are you being faithful to the assigned course of treatment?

4. Addictions

    a. Do you drink alcohol? How much?

    b. Has this interfered with your daily tasks?

    c. Have others expressed concern over how much you are drinking?

    d. Do you take illegal drugs or misuse prescription drugs? How often?

    e. Has this interfered with your daily tasks?

    f. Have others expressed concern over behavior that might be drug related?

    g. Are you having sex outside of marriage? How often? How many partners?

    h. Do you look at pornography? How often?

    i. Do you find sexual thoughts interfere with your daily tasks?

    j. Has a spouse or a friend expressed concern about your sexual behavior?

    k. What other addictive behaviors do you have? For example, gambling, workaholism, extravagant spending.

    l. Has a spouse or a friend expressed concern about this behavior?

    m. Have you seen a mental health provider about any of these? If so, what did he/she say?

    n. Are you being faithful to the assigned course of treatment?

Possession

Traditionally, possession is thought to be the inhabiting of the victim by a demon residing in the place where the Spirit of God would otherwise reside. Others (such as Gabriele Amorth)[6] have expanded the understanding of possession to mean that the victim's will is under the control of the demonic forces occasionally, frequently, or constantly. Thus, it would seem that the question of whether or not a Christian can be possessed is a matter of definition. Certainly, according to the first definition, a Christian cannot be possessed. Yet, from the perspective of the second understanding, the history of the church is replete with examples.[7] It is likely that both kinds of attack exist, and from a pastoral perspective it is

---

6. Amorth, *An Exorcist Tells His Story,* 33, 91-92.

7. Ibid., 56-58, 64-65.

not constructive to quibble over the definitions of terms, especially since the term "possession" does not occur in the Bible.

Some authors speak of various kinds of possessions. They may be constant or seemingly temporary.[8] They may affect all thoughts and behaviors or influence only certain ones. A person may be possessed against his will or he may have willingly invited the demon. In the latter case, unless the victim is ready to disinvite the demon, exorcism is typically useless for this person. Only concerted prayer over a long time and the miraculous intervention of God is of any use in this case.

Diagnostic Considerations

1. In general, if the following behaviors occur, then a diagnosis of possession is probably indicated:

   a. Unnatural strength, such as the ability to move enormous weight or successfully resist efforts at restraint from a much larger, stronger person.

   b. Levitation or psychokinesis (moving objects without physical contact).

   c. Automatic or spirit writing (writing coherent messages while unconscious).

   d. Knowledge of events far away or in the future that the person could not know.

   e. Ability to speak in a language not previously known by the person (which, of course, must be distinguished from the Godly spiritual gift of speaking in an unknown tongue).

   f. Violent reactions to coming in contact with blessed objects (e.g., a cross, stole, holy oil, or holy water) when the person could not be aware of the object's presence. For example, one way to diagnose possession would be to give the unaware victim a glass of holy water to

8. Ibid., 92.

drink.[9] If it is prepared in accordance with the instructions that follow in the next section, only a possessed person should react violently to it. This is not to say that someone who does not react violently is not demonized as the demon could leave temporarily. Note: never drink holy water from a font or any other open container as it may be infected. Use only freshly blessed water stored in a clean container.

2. While bizarre and even blasphemous behavior (such as cursing or defiling holy objects), hearing voices, speaking in an unnatural tone, or hallucinations *might* be symptomatic of possession, it is more likely to be a sign of mental or medical health problems. No person should be diagnosed as being possessed without having a thorough medical exam by an internist or family practitioner and a mental health assessment by a psychologist or psychiatrist. Likewise, unless you are a properly qualified professional, do not make medical or psychological diagnoses.

3. It is very important for the exorcist to watch for multiple infestations of demonic spirits.

   a. This is especially true of someone who has been demonically attacked for a number of years. As our Lord tells us in Luke 11:26, weaker demons may open the way for stronger demons. This process may go on for some time.

   b. The minister should be aware that the stronger demons may force the weaker to identify themselves. Once the lesser are cast out, the greater spirits often cause the possession to go on for a while without symptoms in order to lull the victim, friends and family, and the minister

---

9. Conversely, one way to rule out possession may be to undertake a *ruse de guerre* and give a person a glass of ordinary water or splash them with ordinary water and tell them it is holy water. A demon will know it is not and likely will not react violently. However, be aware that the demon may engage in a *ruse de guerre* of his own. See Amorth, *An Exorcist Tells His Story,* 120-121.

into a false sense that a complete deliverance has been achieved.

    c. It is for this reason that the rite of exorcism can take so long and may have to be performed a number of times.

Diagnostic Questions

1. Questions for the Victim

    a. Do you think you are possessed? Why?

    b. Have you been behaving strangely of late (for example, sudden, uncharacteristic urges or anything that you normally do not do)? In what way?

    c. Have you noticed any unusual events occurring around you, such as objects moving or animals behaving strangely?

    d. Have you heard voices? How would you describe them? What were they saying? Did they seem to be arising from within (for example, in your own mind) or from without (for example, as though someone is in the room conversing with you)? How did you respond to them? Were other people present? How did they respond?[10]

    e. Have you seen unusual things? How would you describe them? How did you respond to them? Were others present? How did they respond?

    f. Have you experienced other sensory events, that is, something you smelled, tasted, or touched? How would you describe them? How did you respond to them? Were others present? How did they respond?

2. Questions for Observers

    a. Do you think the victim is possessed? Why?

10. Be careful to distinguish demonic sensory phenomena from hallucinations of psychopathological origin—get your mental health professional involved.

b. Has he/she been behaving strangely of late (for example, sudden, uncharacteristic urges or anything that he/she normally do not do)? In what way?

c. Have you noticed any unusual events occurring around him/her, such as objects moving or animals behaving strangely?

d. Does he/she report hearing voices? How does he/she describe them? What are the voices saying? Does the victim say that they seem to be arising from within (for example, in his/her own mind) or from without (for example, as though someone is in the room conversing with him/her)? How does he/she respond to them? Do you or anyone else present besides the victim ever hear anything unusual? Please describe it. How do you or they respond?

e. Has the victim reported seeing unusual things? How did he/she describe them? How did he/she respond to them? Were you or others present? Did you or anyone else besides the victim see anything unusual? Please describe it. How did you or they respond?

f. Are there other sensory events, that is, something you or others present besides the victim smell, taste, or touch? How would you or how did they describe it? How did the victim respond to these events? Were you or others present? Please describe it. How did you or they respond?

Hauntings

Every Christian family should want their house blessed, ensuring wicked spirits are driven from the house and the Holy Spirit is invited to come into their home. There are a number of liturgical sources available for this, especially in connection with house blessings performed at Epiphanytide and Eastertide.

Sometimes people will report that their house is haunted—strange, unexplained events are happening that are disquieting to them. Without going into the various theories as to the nature of a haunting, it is sometimes true that evil entities become attached to a location, particularly if some violent act was committed there or if an especially evil person lived there, in essence "consecrating" (setting apart for special use or spiritual ownership) the location for the demonic. In general, though, it is a good idea to recommend that a competent contractor or building inspector inspect the home to rule out any structural, mechanical, electrical, or plumbing problems. This will in no way interfere with performing a house-cleansing liturgy.

Diagnostic Considerations

1. A cleansing ritual is definitely indicated if one or more of the following are taking place:

   a. Objects moving by themselves with an apparent intelligent intent (movement is not random but rather appears purposeful), or appearing or disappearing apparently by themselves.

   b. Unexplained fires or utility failures (but first rule out electrical, plumbing, mechanical, or structural failures).

   c. Seeing ghostly or demonic figures or hearing unsettling sounds that have an apparently intelligent origin—that is, a meaningful, often malevolent interaction with family members or guests.

   d. Other sensory phenomena that defy logical explanation, such as offensive odors, changes in atmospheric pressure, and strangely cold or hot areas, that suddenly appear and disappear or that have a definite boundary, that is, there is no gradual increase or decrease in intensity as something of natural origin would have (that is, there is no diffusion).

2. The ritual <u>may</u> be required if one or more of these are present, but note that these probably (but not necessarily) have a non-supernatural origin.

   a. Objects moving by themselves, but without apparent intelligent intent.

   b. Ill health in the family.

   c. Strong unpleasant odors or other sensory phenomena which do not meet the conditions stated above.

   d. Unsettling sights or sounds that do not seem to have an intelligent origin.

   e. A sense of unease, disquiet, or agitation.

Note that many of these phenomena may have natural explanations and these should be ruled out. For example, a house with faulty wiring may release a substantial amount of electromagnetic energy into the house. This has been shown to cause ill health and a sense of fear or oppression with no clear reason. An electrician with the appropriate equipment can quickly determine whether or not this is the case and, if so, fix the problem

Spiritual attacks manifesting themselves as a haunting may not be attached to the house itself. Sometimes objects and even people can be the source of such events. Cursed objects—things having a demonic attachment—and demonically attacked people may be the cause. This is when the gift of discernment is especially useful.

Be aware that cursed objects may not appear to be significant. Cursed objects (including hex items, see below) are items that are "consecrated" for the demonic. Cult or occult objects, such as Masonic rings, totems, or pentagrams, are obvious candidates for consideration. Even familiar objects that have been passed down through generations or gifts that are seemingly innocent, and even bits of sticks and string (hex items, often tied together in a peculiar manner) may be material foci for curses.

It is possible to cleanse some items through holy water and prayer. Items with obvious occult connections or that serve no meaningful purpose (hex items) should be identified and destroyed through burning or crushing and disposing[11] of the residue by scattering or throwing away in the trash (the last only if destroyed—merely throwing an object away is not sufficient). Under no circumstances should these things or portions of them (such as a gemstone from a ring) be left intact and kept, passed on to others, or merely thrown away in the trash. Appropriate prayers of exorcism or cleansing should be said in dealing with cursed objects.

Curses

Curses are the demonic counterpart of blessings. In the West we often underestimate or even deprecate the power of the occult to bring misfortune into the lives of others. Yet, the Bible and the experience of the ancient Church make this clear—curses are real. Witches and sorcerers are real. The power of evil to negatively impact the well-being of others is real.

Occult practitioners[12] often attack their victims through the use of hex items. Hex items are in effect targeting systems that call the attention of demons to the intended victim.[13] They are often made with some part of the victim's body (e.g., hair, nail trimmings, or blood), in the image (usually a rough image) of the victim, or according to an intricate design, perhaps with one or more arcane ingredients. This may sound strange and superstitious, but reputable, educated exorcists have reported these objects are common in the case of demonic attacks.[14]

---

11. It is not unknown for strange things to occur while this is happening. Be prepared.

12. For example, witches, warlocks, sorcerers, practitioners of "white" or "black" magic, Wiccans, Satanists, or neo-pagans. Clergy I interviewed have told many stories about occult practitioners deliberately targeting Christians, especially ministers.

13. A sort of corrupted sacrament in which material objects are used to bring about curses, much like the true sacraments are used to bring about blessings.

14. See, for example, Amorth, *An Exorcist Tells His Story,* 138-140.

Diagnostic Questions

1. Occult Activity:

   a. Are you or have you in the past been involved in any kind of occult activity, including witchcraft, sorcery, Satanism, Wicca, tarot cards, Ouija board, horoscopes, or fortune telling?

   b. Is someone you know involved in any of these activities?

2. Occult Enemies:

   a. Is there someone you would call an enemy? Who is it? For what reason?

   b. Have you crossed or otherwise hindered someone? In what way?

   c. Is there someone in your circle of acquaintances that causes you a sense of unease?

3. Cursed Objects:

   a. Are you in possession of objects with occult or pagan connections, such as Buddha statues, Masonic rings, or pentagrams?

   b. Have you found any strange objects in your home, place of work, or other locations where you are commonly found? What did these objects look like?

   c. Have you seen someone in possession of that object or one similar to it?

Family Curses and Maledictions

Even more devastating than occult curses and maledictions are those of family origin. These can range from a general wish or statement of ill-will—"You'll never amount to anything," to indirect curses—"If you marry that woman, nothing good will come of it," to direct curses—"I hope you'll just die," to occultic maledictions such as Masonic blood oaths.

These curses involve familiar spirits (that is, spirits which appear to be assigned to infect a particular family, often for generations) and are difficult to break. That said, the minister must be careful to distinguish between emotional abuse through the power of suggestion and self-fulfilling prophecies from genuine curses (though these cannot necessarily be separated).

Indeed, the strongholds of familiar spirits are hard to destroy because they may grow stronger as generations pass. Several exorcists of my acquaintance believe that the origins of this family-level demonic stronghold may be very difficult to trace. However, they may be identifiable based upon patterns of destructive behaviors that tend to run in the family.

As a personal example, I had a continuing struggle with unreasonable anger. A search in the family history showed that this was a recurring problem, with records going all the way back to medieval Scotland! With the advice of Christians with the gift of discernment and through a combination of multiple prayers of deliverance by anointed ministers, medical treatment for cyclothymia (a mood disorder), and counseling, I found a great degree of liberty. As I mentioned before, it is common for spiritual, mental, and emotional health conditions to be intertwined.

Renouncing family curses (the opposite of blessings) and maledictions (the opposite of benedictions) should be done by the person under attack him or herself in front of at least two witnesses not of his or her family, although the additional presence of family members is often beneficial. At least one of the witnesses should be a trained minister of deliverance. It may also be helpful to burn or otherwise destroy some family object associated with the person(s) who is (are) associated with instigating or perpetuating the curse or malediction.

Care must be taken in distinguishing between a true curse or malediction from "bad blood" between family members, though both may be present at the same time.

Diagnostic Considerations[15]—Is there a family or personal history of:

1. Violence, violent crime, abuse.

2. Freemasonry, witchcraft, astrology, tarot cards, Ouija boards, fortune telling, horoscopes, obsession with horror/occult movies and books.

3. Atheism, agnosticism, Mormonism, Oneness Pentecostalism, Jehovah's Witnesses, any non-Christian or pseudo-Christian cult or religion, theological liberalism, heresy, and false religion.

4. Cardiovascular disease, cancer, depression, schizophrenia, bi-polar, obsessive-compulsive disorder.

5. Alcoholism, drug addiction, compulsive gambling, sex addictions, compulsive lying, perfectionism.

6. Adultery, infidelity, fornication, homosexuality (gay and lesbian), other disordered sexual behavior, debauchery (excessive partying), dishonest or immoral business practices, pollution or misuse of creation.

Summary

1. Demonic attacks can be difficult to diagnose.

2. Medical and mental health professionals, as well as friends and family need to be involved.

3. Demonic attacks may be thought of as five types:

    a. Oppression—an attack against the victim's wellbeing

15. These are not necessarily demonic activities, but they *may* be indicators of such.

    b. Obsession—an attack on the victim's thoughts and emotions through unnatural attraction or focus.

    c. Possession—an attack on the victim's will.

    d. Haunting—an attack through the victim's home.

    e. Curses—an attack that originates through ill-will directed toward the victim or a spiritual inheritance of evil.

4. Use careful diagnostic procedures including the SOAP method and other questions and considerations.

5. Keep good records.

6. Pray without ceasing.

2

Deliverance Ministry: Practical Aspects

Introduction

IN GENERAL TERMS, DELIVERANCE ministry is an action of the Church—through her authorized representatives who are appropriately gifted by the Holy Spirit—to pray for and counsel someone who is demonically attacked so that the person may live in the freedom which comes with being a son or a daughter of God. This ministry includes general prayers of intercession; specific, targeted prayers of protection; concerted, Spirit-empowered prayers attacking demonic forces; acts of worship (for example the various litanies for deliverance as well as Holy Communion); and finally the rite of exorcism (if required).

Typically, a minister will make a determination of the need for deliverance after an initial meeting with the victim through the steps listed earlier. Perhaps he/she will also discern the need to pray for and counsel the victim at that meeting. Under most circumstances, deliverance may proceed under the same sorts of due diligence procedures and conditions that the minister would follow for pastoral counseling. That said, more severe forms of demonic attack are best handled by a team.

The Deliverance Ministry Team

Building the Team

When should you form a deliverance ministry team? Now! Don't wait until one is needed. It takes time to recruit and train an effective team.

The question of who should be involved in deliverance ministry and in what capacity is not as easy as it first appears. The team can be as simple as including a discerning friend or as structured as an exorcism team. In general, if an instance of demonic attack is more involved than that requiring the simple encouragement and counsel of a friend or pastor, then a team of two or more people should be involved.

The task of leading a deliverance team should be assigned to the pastor of the victim or someone authorized by the pastor, and, in the case of exorcism, only someone authorized by the pastor's bishop or other similar Church authority.[1] This appointment

---

1. Such as a presbytery or district superintendent.

should be based upon his or her gifting, maturity in the faith, submission to authority, and experience in spiritual warfare.

The pastor should be wary of people who self-identify as expert warriors—history has often shown that these are too often spiritual thrill-seekers and self-promoters who want the seeming glamour of such a ministry. The fact of the matter is that there is nothing glamorous about this ministry. Indeed, the less well known a spiritual warfare minister is the better. Pride is too often a besetting sin in this arena of ministry. The model here is not a knight in shining armor riding out onto a battlefield before an admiring army to challenge the enemy to single combat, but rather one of a covert operative whose role and identity are known only to the few who have a need to know. This cannot be said too often—beware of the sin of pride: it will destroy. More on the composition of the team may be found in chapter 3.

Spiritual Gifts

Certain spiritual gifts are absolutely critical for deliverance ministry. No one will likely have all of them, so a variety of people will need to be recruited. The kinds of gifts the pastor should look for in someone who has the potential for this ministry are:

1. Discernment: Detect and identify spirits.

2. Faith and Healing: Believe that God will intervene by strengthening the minister and team and healing the victim.

3. Knowledge: Know and understand the ways, means, reasons, and motivations of the demonic attack.

4. Wisdom: Determine how best to deal with a particular case of demonic attack.

5. Pastor: Lead the team and care for both the victim and the team.

Again, it is unlikely that someone will have all of these gifts, which is why working in teams is often necessary.

Mentoring

If the pastor does identify someone who is a likely candidate for deliverance ministry, then that person should be assigned a mentor who is an experienced member of a deliverance ministry team with similar gifting. The mentor should report to the pastor regularly on the candidate's progress. The candidate may participate in deliverance ministry only under the supervision of his/her mentor. Only after training and at least one year of experience should the candidate be considered ready to take on a primary role on the team.

The mentor should be trained in the art of mentoring. Knowledge and experience of deliverance ministry is a must, but knowing how to be a good mentor is also important.

Training

Basic training for someone new to deliverance ministry should include the following:

1. Basic knowledge of the Bible and Christian doctrine (to distinguish truth from error).

2. Instruction in the nature of evil and biblical demonology.

3. Self-care for deliverance team members (see chapter 4).

4. The Anglican approach to deliverance ministry (this manual will hopefully suffice).

5. The importance of prayer and fasting.

6. Knowledge of good, basic literature on this subject. I suggest John Richards, *Exorcism, Deliverance and Healing*; Michael Scanlan, *Deliverance from Evil Spirits*; Francis McNutt, *Deliverance from Evil Spirits*; and Leanne Payne, *The Healing Presence* and *Restoring the Christian Soul*.

Advanced training for someone preparing to be a mentor and trainer should include:

1. Methods of mentoring.

2. Familiarity with advanced literature on the subject. I recommend Merrill Unger, *Biblical Demonology;* Kurt E. Koch, *Demonology Past and Present;* and T. Craig Isaacs, *Revelations and Possessions.*

3. Attendance at an outside training course, such as those held by the McNutts or Neal Lozano would be especially beneficial.

Additionally, if there is no qualified medic present (as described in chapter 1) someone on the deliverance ministry team should have current training in Basic Cardiac Life Support (popularly known as CPR) and first aid.

Mechanics and Logistics

There are various means and methods, together with certain supplies, which Scripture and the experience of the Church have found to be efficacious in deliverance ministry.

The Sign of the Cross

Making the sign of the cross is indicated in several of the liturgies included in this manual. Unless otherwise indicated by the instructions, wherever † appears, the sign of the cross may be made over the person or substance being blessed or prayed over. Unless otherwise indicated, the cross may be signed by holy water, holy oil, or by just the hand itself.

Holy Oil and Holy Water

Many of the rites and ceremonies discussed in this manual require the use of holy oil for healing or holy water. According to ancient custom (which, while not infallible, is authoritative), the oil should be blessed or sanctified by a bishop. An exception may be made—in an emergency—for the blessing of oil for one who is ill and expected to die and there is no holy oil available. Oil containing certain spices mentioned in the scripture may be obtained from many Christian supply stores. Pure virgin olive oil may be used as well. The minister may either obtain the oil directly from the bishop or have the bishop bless the church's supply when he next visits the parish.

Traditionally, a priest may bless water. A suggested rite is given in appendix B. Indeed, theoretically, since any Christian may baptize someone in the absence of a priest or deacon, and since holy water is an element that has its sacramental significance in its connection with baptism, any baptized Christian may bless or sanctify water *if there is no priest available.* Holy water combines pure water with a very small amount (a pinch, the smallest amount which can be held between the thumb and forefinger) of salt.[2] Salt has an ancient connection with the sacrament of baptism in that a pinch of salt was placed in the baptizand's mouth, "to signify the spiritual salt, which is the Word of God, wherewith he should be seasoned."[3]

It is interesting to note that, in some traditions (such as the Eastern Orthodox),[4] believers are encouraged to regularly drink holy water, especially those who are struggling against demonic attack. While this should never take the place of receiving the Eucharist (the true "food and drink of new and unending life"), there is no harm and likely much good that may come from this practice if the holy water is from a clean source, freshly consecrated, and stored in a sanitized container.[5]

Prayers and Rites

Prayers of deliverance (see appendix C) may be offered by a priest (preferably) or by some lay minister authorized by his or her pastor on behalf of the victim under attack by demonic powers. The minister should observe the reactions of the victim during the

2. This is an ancient practice attested to by Augustine, *Confessions*, 1.11.

3. Strype, *Ecclesiastical Memorials*, 414–415.

4. St. John Maximovitch, "Selected Sermons, Part II."

5. As a warning, see Associated Press, "117 Hospitalized after Drinking Holy Water."

prayers as they may be of diagnostic value for both pastoral care and for the possible need for exorcism. For example, if the person acts startled at the mention of the pain caused by the death of loved ones, this presents a further area of exploration. Observe the victim's body language during deliverance sessions, especially the eyes, the face, and the hands. Anointing the head with blessed oil or holy water and making the sign of the cross during these prayers is of very great benefit.

Tradition recommends that the minister wear a purple stole (purple being the liturgical color of penitence and the stole representing the authority of the priest) and place one end of it across the neck of the one for whom the prayers are offered. Wearing a surplice is likewise recommended by many authorities and, together with the stole, is canonically required in some exorcism rites.

A single prayer of deliverance is sometimes not sufficient (as our Lord noted in Matt 17:21), especially for generational curses, familiar spirits, and for multiple infestations. It is common for the evil spirits to gradually reveal themselves over time, forcing more minor entities to surface first before the more powerful ones emerge. Also, because of the habitual nature of sinful responses to demonic oppression, it is very easy for the person to be open to re-infestation after deliverance until such time as the mental health issues are addressed. Based upon my research, I recommend at least weekly prayers of deliverance—battles, if you will—for the first few months of warfare and then regular follow-ups. Additionally, the person may require follow up mental health counseling to deal with disordered behavior that often arises from demonization.

Note that prayers of deliverance, and even exorcisms themselves, are ineffective in the long term unless the demonized person commits his or her life to Christ, regularly receives the means of grace, and grows in Christ-like character. Accountability to help growth in faithfulness is as important (if not more so) as any prayer or rite. If at all possible, the victim should profess faith in Christ and be baptized prior to receiving any deliverance ministry.

Suggested prayers of deliverance are included in appendix C of this manual. A suggested form for renouncing family curses and maledictions is found in appendix D. Appendix E is a suggested rite for house cleansing and blessing.

Supplies

The following supplies are recommended

1. Holy oil in a small bottle or container.

2. A purificator for cleaning excess oil.

3. Holy water in a container that allows easy sprinkling.

4. A purple stole.

5. A white surplice (usually optional, but required in some church canons).

6. Bibles and copies of the Book of Common Prayer.

7. Communion ware and elements.

8. A cross.

Additional items for prolonged deliverance/exorcisms

1. Bottles of drinking water.

2. High-energy snacks.

3. Blankets, cushions, and pillows.

4. Medical kit (an wilderness emergency responder kit, available from most outdoor supply stores, is especially good).

5. Cleaning supplies.

Space

The best space for deliverance ministry depends on the nature of the attack. For most sessions, use an office in the church, with appropriate safeguards like open windows or a family member or a person of the same sex as the victim seated outside the office.

Other suitable spaces may be the sanctuary, the house of the victim, or a public area such as a restaurant (for initial meetings only). Privacy and security are equally important.

The room should be appropriately lit and the temperature and air movement should be comfortable to the victim. There should be suitable seating—comfortable, but easy to get in and out of. Adequate and nearby restroom facilities are an often overlooked necessity—be sure they are available.

Legal Aspects

Obtaining informed consent from the victim (or the parents or guardians of a minor), according to a friend of mine who is both a civil and canon lawyer, is of doubtful *legal* benefit, given the litigious nature of our culture. Nevertheless, for ecclesiastical accountability, having a signed consent form is a good idea, as would be a Confidentiality Statement. A sample statement is found in appendix F. The following items should be included:

1. All personal information of the victim will remain confidential except as stipulated in the document.

2. Permission for the minister to perform rites, offer prayers, and counsel the victim.

3. Permission for the minister to inform the victim's pastor (if different than the minister) and the minister's bishop.

4. Permission for the minister and the victim's physician and mental health provider to release information and consult together on those matters related to the victim's health and welfare.

5. Permission to consult other ministers provided the victim's personal information remains confidential.

6. Either the victim or the minister has the right to cease involvement in the deliverance ministry, temporarily or permanently.

7. All matters will be handled in accordance with the Scriptures and the doctrinal and sacramental norms of the minister's Church.

8. The victim has the right to an explanation for any and all aspects of the deliverance ministry.

The minister and everyone on the ministry team who is involved must understand that strict confidentiality must be maintained. They should indicate their understanding by signing the Confidentiality Statement, agreeing to abide by its provisions.

Summary

There are a number of practical considerations that the minister must keep in mind:

1. Give very careful consideration to the calling and motivation of anyone assigned to the deliverance team.

2. Determine the kinds of gifts, skills, and experience the team needs.

3. Consider training and mentoring needs; arrange for the training sessions and the mentoring relationships.

4. Determine what rites should be used.

5. Check to see that the proper supplies are on hand.

6. Ensure there is an appropriate space for the deliverance ministry.

7. Make sure that the victim, the minister, and the deliverance team has read, understood, and signed the Informed Consent and Confidentiality Form.

3

Exorcism

Introduction

ACCORDING TO ANCIENT CUSTOM and practice of the Church, typically only a priest, appointed by his bishop ordinary, should perform the rite of exorcism. However, up until at least the fourth century, specially trained lay exorcists were authorized to perform this ministry. Apparently this was a common practice in the

Eastern Church in the first four or five centuries, but eventually lay exorcists became quite rare.[1] In any event, an exorcist should only perform the rite with the specific authority of his bishop.

It may be rightly asked, "Why does the exorcism take so long? Wouldn't a single, short prayer be sufficient?" Jesus tells us in Matthew 17:21 that a simple prayer is not always effective. Exorcism works on a number of levels, one of which is to cause the evil spirit extreme pain, so that the flames of hell seem (for a while at least) preferable to being in the middle of an exorcism. By conditioning the wicked one to associate pain with the one being delivered, the spirit will be made reluctant to return. Also, as noted in chapter 2, when there are multiple infestations, it may take a great deal of time to remove each layer of demonic inhabitants.

It is absolutely necessary for you and your team to spend the day before an exorcism in fasting and prayer. However, do not fast on the day of the exorcism itself—you and your team will need all the energy you can get.

One final note before we get to the meat of exorcism: exorcisms are not Hollywood scenes. While occasionally something really spectacular may happen, most exorcists report that the rite is considerably less dramatic and much more work than any film portrays.

The Exorcism Team

What sort of people should be on an exorcism team?[2] First of all, there is the priest or specially licensed lay minister who is authorized by the bishop (in Anglicanism often known as the

---

1. Prior to 1972, there was the minor order of exorcist in the Roman Catholic Church. It may have originated in North Africa in the third or fourth centuries (Tertullian, *Apology,* 23; Origen, *Againt Celsus,* 7.4) and was certainly authorized by canon law in the sixth century, as seen in the *Statuta Ecclesiæ Antiqua.* See Toner, "Exorcist." See also Papademetriou, "Exorcism in the Orthodox Church."

2. Having an exorcism team is by far the best approach. However, emergencies may arise, and a team may not be available. The exorcist may have to be flexible but he should still contact his Ordinary.

Ordinary) to lead the team and to serve as the exorcist. He should have experience in spiritual warfare. His focus should be on leading the team, saying the liturgy, and performing the ritual actions. He should be the only person who addresses the victim and the demon(s). Other clergy may assist him. It is especially useful if this assistant is apprenticing for the ministry of exorcism. Also, the assisting clergy can take over for the primary exorcist when he becomes tired and needs a break.

Second, there should be at least one person with the spiritual gift of discernment to monitor the event and report to the priest his or her impressions. It is important that he or she observe the proceedings closely, speak only to the priest or his assistant, and otherwise remain silent.

Third, there should be as many intercessors (prayer warriors) as possible. It is not necessary for them to be present in the room where the exorcism is taking place—indeed it is preferable that they be in another room so that they may pray aloud without distracting or being distracted. If they believe they have received a word of knowledge, wisdom, or discernment from the Lord, it should be conveyed to one of the assisting clergy with as little disturbance as possible, preferably in writing.

Fourth, as previously described, an appropriately trained medic should be present with an emergency medical kit. Additionally, a psychologist or psychiatrist is recommended. If the latter is also ACLS or, better yet, ACLS and ATLS trained, he or she can serve as the attending medic.

Finally, if the exorcist has a reason to suspect the possessed person may become violent and harm him/herself or others present, a strong, steady person to help with physical restraint is a good idea (this can be the assistant or the medic). Do not use manual restraints (such as handcuffs or zip ties) or tie a person to a chair, a bed, or other furniture. Put nothing around the neck, face, chest, or mouth. Be warned, sometimes the victim may have extraordinary strength of demonic origin or even because of mental health issues.[3] In such an instance, several people may be needed

---

3. The demon(s) can be commanded in Jesus' name to stop being violent,

to restrain the victim. Immediately call a halt to the exorcism if adequate safety cannot be maintained.

Also note—under no circumstances should an exorcism be performed on a woman without a female in attendance. There are too many opportunities in such a case for accusations of abuse.

Preparing for the Rite

Legal Statement

An Informed Consent and Confidentiality Statement (found in appendix F) should be signed by the victim if he or she is mentally competent or by a parent or legal guardian. If the victim is not in his/her right mind, and there is no one with the legal right to give permission to perform the rite, you must contact the bishop immediately before proceeding. Additionally, even if the victim is a minor or not mentally competent to make legal decision on his or her behalf, the minister should still explain what is happening to him or her as much as the victim can understand.

Worship

Prior to the exorcism, the priest delegated by the bishop to perform this office, together with the entire team, should participate in the Holy Communion along with the Great Litany. During the service of worship and the rite of exorcism, the presiding priest, with any ordained assistants, should vest in surplice and purple stole. Prior to starting the rite, the priest traces the sign of the cross over himself, the victim, and the bystanders, and then sprinkles all of them with holy water. After this he begins the rite of exorcism.

---

but some mental health factors such as extreme psychotic rage, can make the victim unusually but still naturally strong, at least in the short term. Be careful and remember your immediate priority in such instances is the safety of all involved.

Interactions with Demons

Demons are beings with superior intelligence and guile. They may offer the exorcist knowledge and understanding, trying to distract him from his purpose by luring him into conversation. Demons may also accuse the exorcist of various sins (and anticipate that some of those accusations may be accurate—prior confession and absolution is necessary!) or threaten him or the entire team with dire consequences. The temptation to respond is great, but do not do it. The only conversation you should have with the demon is to demand its name.

Demons may attempt to frighten or distract the exorcist or his team by supernatural feats (e.g., moving things about the room without physical contact), growling, threatening, or violent displays. The exorcist should not tolerate this. He should command such nonsense to cease in the name of Jesus. The exorcist, by God's grace, is deputized by the Lord to be in charge.

The Names of Demons

The name revealed by the demon, when commanded to do so in the name of Jesus Christ, can tell exorcist much about the nature of the spirit with which he is dealing. Without too much speculation on ranks and orders of the demonic hosts, the consensus among Christian demonologists (Amorth is especially helpful here) is that lower ranking demons are often named after vices and sins (e.g., fear, lust, spite, hatred) and higher ranking ones will have biblical names, such as Belial, Azazel, Abaddon, or Baal. Remember that the more powerful demons may force the lesser ones to reveal themselves in order to cover up the presence of the stronger.[4]

---

4. Amorth, *An Exorcist Tells His Story,* 91-92.

After the Conclusion of the Rite

Following the rite, prayers should be said for the team, the victim, all others present, *and their families* for their protection and peace. All should be admonished to exercise care, not out of fear but out of wisdom, when they do anything in which there is a potential for harm such as driving or operating power tools. Additionally, the minister should follow up with all present to check on their welfare. A good practice would be to follow up daily for the first week afterwards and weekly for the next month.

Summary

1. Exorcisms are fearful and wonderful events. By the power of the Spirit, they set souls free. No exorcism should be performed lightly.

2. Great care should be taken in the selection of the exorcism team.

3. Prepare for the rite thoroughly.

4. Do not engage demons in conversation. Be intolerant of any nonsense they might try. You have authority in Jesus' name.

5. Do not fear the demons' pretense at power or majesty. Only God is all-powerful, and to him alone belongs the majesty, glory, honor, power, might, and dominion, unto the eternal ages.

4

Pastoral Care

Introduction

PEOPLE WHO ARE CALLED by God into deliverance ministry are under special surveillance by Satan, especially after setting someone free from the devil's attacks. Likewise, the victim who has been delivered will come under renewed attack as the demons try to reclaim one whom they regarded as their own. Also keep in mind the possibility of attacks on the families of the ministers, the team, and the victim. How do you deal with these attacks?

Self-Care for the Minister

By minister in this instance, I mean all the people involved on the deliverance team, even the medic and a person who helped in restraining a victim during an exorcism. In the sense that they all ministered or served (in the Greek, *diakoneisis*), they are all ministers.

Preventive Care

As with physical health, the best way to prevent damage from the attacks of the enemy is to take care of yourself. All humans are an integrated whole with body, mind, emotions, will, spirit, and social components. Whatever promotes health in one component will positively affect the others.

Physical

Stay in shape, eat right, see your doctor and dentist regularly, and get plenty of sleep. Exercise for at least 30 minutes a day, four or five days a week. You do not have to be a "fitness fanatic," but by following this regimen you will increase your endurance and reduce the numbers of chinks in your physical "armor."

Mental and emotional

Learn to self-talk through problems. Here is a routine that I use:

1. What is going on?

2. Is this internal (something I'm thinking or feeling) or external (something that's happening to me)?

3. If it's internal, is this a thought or an emotion?

4. If it's a thought, is this thought true, honorable, just, pure, lovely, commendable, excellent, praiseworthy? (Phil 4:8) If so, should I act on it? If not, how can I take this thought captive to obey Christ? (2 Cor 10:5)

5. If it's an emotion, does it reflect the love of God which is in Christ Jesus? (Eph 5:2) Is it fear? (2 Tim 1:7; 1 John 4:18) How am I not trusting God so that it lead to this fear? Is it anger? Is the anger justified by the circumstances? Will acting on this anger help the situation? If not, how can I dissipate or resolve the anger? (Eph 4:26; Jam 1:19) Is it guilt or shame? Why? (Rom 5:5; 8:1-2)

It is crucial that you have two or three people in your life with whom you can share your heart and mind, having confidence in their love, support, and counsel. If your thoughts or emotions seem to run away with you, do not be afraid or ashamed to seek the advice of a Christian mental health professional (but choose a therapist who believes in deliverance ministry—consult a senior priest or your bishop if you do not know of such a professional).

Sexual

It seems obvious, but too many ministering in deliverance ministry are attacked in the area of sexual thoughts and behaviors. Practice biblical sexual purity. If you are married, sexual purity means having a healthy sex life with your spouse every bit as much as it means abstaining from inappropriate sexual thinking and activities.

Spiritual

This may seem self-evident, but it is surprising how often those in deliverance ministry neglect their own soul's health. Stay in the Word, pray, and worship every day. Hear the Word taught and preached and receive Holy Communion at least weekly. Take time out at least a couple of times a year to get away from your duties and stresses, spending time alone with God.

Here is a daily routine I follow.

1. Say the daily offices and read the lectionary texts. If you miss the morning or the evening office, say the office of compline. I use http://www.churchofengland.org/prayer-worship/join-us-in-daily-prayer.aspx. In this way, you are praying and worshipping at least twice a day and are also reading four Bible chapters (or major portions of chapters) and several psalms.

2. I exercise alone so that, especially when I'm on the treadmill or walking, I can pray extemporaneously. I sometimes use Anglican prayer beads, with each bead representing some area of concern.

3. This is something I'm not terribly good at, but I'm seeking to get better—during every transition point in the day, for example, shifting from task to another, say a short prayer, asking God for wisdom, knowledge, and discernment.

I also recommend that you get together with some of the members of your team and pray regularly some of the prayers of deliverance found in appendix C over one another. Sometimes, when the fight gets dirty, spiritual "dirt" (e.g., an oppressing spirit) can cling to you without your awareness. Finally, find a spiritual director, accountability partner, or confessor to meet with regularly.

Social

I am by nature an introvert, although I can act like an extrovert when needed. It is easy for me to hole-up somewhere, especially after a trying day, and sit by myself. That's okay, but the fellowship of others is important. Set aside regular times of feasting and fun with friends and family. Enjoy good food and wine (neither to excess). Watch an uplifting movie with someone. Play scrabble. Do not be a hermit—it's easy to enter into a dark place in the mind and heart without some fun in your life.

The Power of Prayer in Self-Deliverance

You feel a headache coming on and take aspirin or ibuprofen. You detect the tickle in your throat, the burning in your eyes, and the impending sneeze and take an over-the-counter antihistamine. You sense the pain and pressure of heartburn welling up inside of you and take an antacid. In the same way, you sense that something is not right spiritually and do something about it. Just as the drug store has shelves full of medications with proven effectiveness, there are a number of spiritual treatments available to the individual Christian for the purpose of healing.

Prayer

In essence, all useful self-medications come down to the means of grace that are actually forms of prayer.

The Discipline of Daily Prayer and Scripture Reading

This has already been mentioned, but it is worth repeating. Just as exercise, eating well, taking vitamins, and sleeping seven to eight hours a night will help prevent disease, so the daily discipline of prayer and scripture reading are preventative practices against many forms of spiritual attack. Note, however, that any Christian who is so disciplined will be a threat to the devil and will draw various kinds of attacks. Vitamins make it harder for the cold virus to infect us, but not impossible. Disciplines make it harder for us to be demonically assaulted, but not impossible.

Types of Prayer

In daily spiritual exercises, there should be three types of prayer: set form or liturgical prayer, extemporaneous prayer, and listening prayer. Using a set form or liturgy assists the Christian in praying for all that God commands us. It is easy to forget to pray for government leaders, for example, when your heart and mind are struggling with a friend's illness, yet we are commanded so to do in 1 Timothy 2:1-2. Extemporaneous prayer allows us to pour our hearts out to God in a transparent manner. Listening prayer reminds us that prayer is communication with God and effective communication is a two-way practice.

Scripture Reading

This aspect should be in two forms: reading for knowledge and understanding (food for the mind) and reading for wisdom (food for the spirit). The former involves systematic study using helps such as lexicons and commentaries. This leads to a deeper knowledge of the content of the text and keener understanding of the meaning of the text. The latter is sometimes called *lectio divina*. This involves slow, prayerful reading of the text to instruct the reader in his or her personal growth in grace, leading to obedience to God's commandments and fervent love for God and His people—in other words, wisdom.

Fasting

Sometimes it is necessary to engage in a more rigorous discipline to sharpen prayers and Scripture reading. One of the biblically prescribed methods is fasting. Here are some guidelines.

1. Seasons and times:

    a. Fast or abstain from certain foods or activities during the seasons of Advent (possibly) and Lent (definitely) and the day before a major feast.

    b. Many Christians follow the practice of fasting lunch on Wednesday and abstaining from certain foods (such as meat) on Fridays.

    c. Consider fasting one meal a day or fasting from sunup to sundown for a season.

2. If you fast from all food:

   a. Never fast for more than 72 hours without checking with your physician.

   b. Consider drinking fruit juice if you are fasting from food.

   c. Always stay well hydrated. If your urine isn't clear or a very pale straw color, you're not drinking enough. If you do not drink enough water during fasting, you can become very ill.

   d. Avoid doing vigorous activity, especially physical labor or exercise.

   e. If this is your first time attempting such a fast, avoid driving or operating heavy equipment, or making important decisions until you learn how fasting affects you.

3. If you fast from some kinds of food, drink, or activities:

   a. Abstaining from something you should not eat, drink, or do anyway is not a fast.

   b. If you drink more than one or two caffeinated beverages a day, fasting from caffeine will be very hard on everyone. Count the cost.

   c. You should fast from something that is good or enjoyable (but not sinful) for you such as watching television, reading mystery novels, eating chocolate, and so forth.

   d. If you are married, get your spouse's permission before abstaining from sexual activity. Follow Paul's instructions in 1 Corinthians 7:1-5.

4. Anytime you fast, replace the time gained with an additional spiritual discipline, such as spending more time in prayer or reading Scripture.

It is sometimes the case, especially when fasting from all food, that you will not notice the benefit until after the fast is over.

Prayer of Others

If you run a fever that aspirin will not break, you need to go see a doctor. If you are under spiritual attack and the self-care does not work, get a few members of the deliverance ministry team together and have them pray some of the prayers of deliverance over you. Don't just wait until you're under attack—do this regularly as prevention.

Self-Care and Follow-Up Care for the Victim

In general, the victim should follow everything said above concerning the self-care of the members of a deliverance ministry team after he or she is freed from demonic attack. However, there are some additional steps.

1. The minister should regularly follow-up with the victim and run through the diagnostic steps and prayers. A good pattern is once a day for the first week, weekly for the next month, monthly for the next year, and annually from then on for as long as the person is under the minister's care.

2. The victim may have health problems that were caused or aggravated by the attack. He or she should see his/her doctor for a physical. A Christian physician is more likely to understand what the victim has been through and work with him/her sympathetically.

3. The victim will often have mental health issues. Bad habits, destructive thinking patterns, and out-of-control emotions are very common. Seeing a Christian counselor is more than likely a necessity.

4. The victim will be tempted to go back into his/her previous lifestyle—it is what he/she knows. This can lead to disastrous consequences (Luke 11:26). Gently push him/her into a new lifestyle that includes self-discipline, regular receiving of the means of grace, and active involvement in in the life of the church.

Summary

1. It is absolutely critical for the deliverance ministry team members to engage in self-care, not only immediately before and after a deliverance session, but also as a lifestyle. This should include maintaining one's physical, mental and emotional, social, and spiritual health.

2. Deliverance team members need to live disciplined lives. This is the best way to prevent or address demonic attacks in their lives.

3. Regular prayer, scripture reading, and receiving the means of grace are essential. So are periodic times of fasting and abstinence.

4. All of this applies to the victim as well. The minister should make every effort reasonable to hold him or her accountable to do this. If the victim is not willing to be accountable (and this is, sadly, not unusual), then he or she should be warned about the likely consequences of this unwillingness.

Two Prayers for Warriors

O almighty and most merciful God, according to your abundant goodness we ask you to keep us from all things that may hurt us, so that we, being ready both in body and soul, may cheerfully accomplish those things which you command; through Jesus Christ our Lord. *Amen.*

We ask you, almighty God, to look upon the heartfelt desires of your humble servants and stretch forth the right hand of your majesty to be our defense against all our enemies; through Jesus Christ our Lord. *Amen.*[1]

---

1. Adapted from *A Prayer Book for Soldiers and Sailors.*

Appendix A

An Example of SOAP

Note: All names, dates, and locations are changed to protect confidentiality.

Name: Janet Jones
Date first seen: June 1, 2010

Subjective Component

Janet Jones is a 50 year-old white female. She has been working for Grady Construction in Memphis, TN since January 2007. She says she's been a Christian since fifth grade and was baptized as an infant. She was raised nominally as a Lutheran and has been attending St. Alban's Anglican Church for about 10 years. She has been married to John for 25 years. It is her first marriage. She has three children, ages 23, 21, and 19.

She indicates that there is a family history of anger and mental illness. She reports struggles in dealing with her still-living, abusive mother. Her mother emotionally abused her children, especially Janet, and said negative things regarding her that she has taken very much to heart.

She indicates she struggles with anxiety, feelings of condemnation and guilt, and anxious dreams that negatively affect her the following morning. She also states that she has problems with easily taking offense at what others say or do toward her (or so she believes). She indicates awareness that this response may be largely inappropriate. She states she has frequent anxiety in social situations, but at other times finds she does well. She is also struggling with a sense of distance from Christ, lack of intimacy, and difficulty in trusting God.

She had surgery for breast cancer, followed by chemotherapy (which ended six months ago) and is now suffering from a relapse/recurrence. This understandably upsets her.

Objective Component

Personal observations

Janet presents as nervous, agitated, and anxious. Her body language sometimes reflects a defensive posture, including crossing her arms and sitting hunched over. She has occasional facial twitches in the form of winks—it is unclear whether she is aware of them or not. She is obviously tired. She has a somewhat formal, controlled demeanor. During an initial meeting which included general prayers of deliverance on June 1, 2010 she reacted by a strong contraction of her frontalis muscle (the forehead) at the mention of family issues and anger.

Prayers used: lesser litany of deliverance, prayer for deliverance against the attacks of the evil one, a prayer for sanctification, a prayer against every evil, a prayer for spiritual healing.

Other observations

Janet was referred to two laywomen with the gift of discernment (Lauren Boyd and Mary Clinch) for a discernment session on June 10. This session revealed issues related to trauma from childhood, unresolved anger, and a lack of forgiveness.

During follow up prayers of deliverance with me on June 15, attended by a chaperone (Mary Clinch) and an observer (the Rev. John Black), the two reported very obvious physical reactions (sudden overall body tensing, tears, and grimacing) at the mention of woundedness from childhood and anger issues.

Assessment

Mental health

Possibilities only, not a diagnosis; will need to refer: post-traumatic stress disorder stemming from childhood abuse?

Spiritual health

Primary: Oppression via family curse

Secondary: Obsession via familiar spirit or spirits (unlikely)

Spiritual disturbance is likely secondary to mental health issues. Deliverance ministry is indicated as an adjunct thereto.

Plan

Mental health

I will advise Janet to see a Christian mental health provider to receive diagnosis and treatment for mental/emotional health issues. This is a critical component and is essential for her healing. I will also advise her that this matter is necessary because when such issues are unaddressed, they can lead to a vulnerability to further attacks.

Spiritual health

Focus of treatment: Christ-centered esteem (Sonship); forgiveness of mother (and father? explore); releasing anger; breaking evil family ties, maledictions, and curses.

I provided her with an individualized daily prayer and Scripture regimen (see below). I will meet with her June 21[1] to see how she feels. I will also schedule additional meetings (two at first) with her for additional prayers of deliverance and also deal directly with the issue of family curses.

Spiritual Self Care Plan for Janet Jones

Pray this on rising in the morning.

Soul of Christ, sanctify me. Body of Christ, save me. Blood of Christ, inebriate me, your servant. Water from the side of Christ, wash me. Passion of Christ, strengthen me. O good Jesus, hear my prayer—within your wounds hide me. Let me never be separate from you. From the evil one, protect me. At the hour of death, call me and bid me come to you that with your saints I may praise you forever. Amen.

Read these aloud before leaving your house in the morning.

Philippians 4:6-8. Do not be anxious about anything, but in everything by prayer and supplication with thanksgiving let your requests be made known to God. And the peace of God, which surpasses all understanding, will guard your hearts and your minds in Christ Jesus. Finally, brothers, whatever is true, whatever is honorable, whatever is just, whatever is pure, whatever is lovely, whatever is commendable, if there is any excellence, if there is anything worthy of praise, think about these things.

1 Peter 2:9. But you are a chosen race, a royal priesthood, a holy nation, a people for his own possession, that you may

1. This meeting indicated that she was being faithful to the disciplines outlined. After three more meetings with good progress, including the development of solid accountability relationships, we agreed to stop meeting. Her cancer went into remission but, within a year after this remission, her cancer returned and she died shortly thereafter.

proclaim the excellencies of him who called you out of darkness into his marvelous light.

Romans 8:1&2. There is therefore now no condemnation for those who are in Christ Jesus. For the law of the Spirit of life has set you free in Christ Jesus from the law of sin and death.

Psalm 119:65. Great peace have they which love your law and nothing shall offend them.

2 Corinthians 6:18. "I will be a father to you, and you shall be sons and daughters to me," says the Lord Almighty.

Galatians 4:1-7. I mean that the heir, as long as he is a child, is no different from a slave, in the same way we also, when we were children, were enslaved to the elementary principles of the world. But when the fullness of time had come, God sent forth his Son, born of woman, born under the law, to redeem those who were under the law, so that we might receive adoption as sons. And because you are sons, God has sent the Spirit of his Son into our hearts, crying, "Abba! Father!" So you are no longer a slave, but a son, and if a son, then an heir through God.

Read every night before retiring.

Psalm 4:8. In peace I will both lie down and sleep; for you alone, O LORD, make me dwell in safety.

O Father, Son, and Holy Spirit, this night I claim the protection of Jesus' blood and the authority of his name, to drive off and banish all demons of the night. Evil dreams, be gone! Nightmares, be gone! All dreams born of anxiety or guilt, be gone! Diabolic attacks against my rest, be gone! Sleep that is restless, be gone! Holy angels, you who have been created to minister to the needs of God's children, surround me tonight. O holy God, the holy and strong, the holy and immortal one, have mercy upon me and give me peace. Amen.

Appendix B

The Blessing of Holy Water

The priest will need the following items: pure table salt in a small saucer, clean water in a pitcher or carafe, and a purple stole. Traditionally the priest would also wear a surplice. The priest says the entire liturgy. If others are present, they may respond by saying everything after the asterisk (*). When † appears in the text, the priest should make the sign of the cross over the indicated element. Instructions are indicated with brackets.

The Exorcism of Salt

My help is in the name of the Lord, * who has made heaven and earth.

[Placing his hand over the salt, the priest says . . .]

I command you, O salt,

In the name of God the † Father Almighty,

In the name of Jesus Christ † his only Son our Lord,

And by the power of the Holy † Spirit,

That you become spiritually clean for the welfare of those who trust in Christ.

Bring health and safety to the bodies and souls of all who receive you.

Let ungodly thoughts; evil in thought, word, and deed; and the wickedness and deceits of the world and the devil flee from your presence:

In the name of Jesus Christ, who shall come again to judge both the living and the dead. * Amen.

The Blessing of Salt

[Keeping his hand over the salt, the priest continues . . .]

Almighty and everlasting God,

I humbly ask you, according to your great and limitless mercy that you, out of your grace, will † bless and † sanctify this salt, that it may bring, to all that take of it, healing of soul, mind, and body.

Let whatever is touched with it be set free from all disease, sinfulness, and assaults of spiritual wickedness, through Jesus Christ our Lord. * Amen.

The Exorcism of Water

[Holding his hand over the water, the priest says . . .]

I command you, O water,

In the name of God the † Father Almighty,

In the name of Jesus Christ † his only Son our Lord,

And by the power of the Holy † Spirit,

That you become spiritually clean for the welfare of those who trust in Christ.

Bring health and safety to the bodies and souls of all who receive you.

Let ungodly thoughts; evil in thought, word, and deed; and the wickedness and deceits of the world and the devil flee from your presence:

In the name of Jesus Christ, who shall come again to judge both the living and the dead. * Amen.

The Blessing of Water

[Keeping his over the water, the priest continues . . .]

Let us pray.

O God, for the salvation of humanity you established that water should be used in the sacrament of baptism:

Graciously look upon us who call upon you, and pour the power of your † blessing upon this water,

That, just as it is suitable for the sacrament of baptism,

It may become a vehicle of divine grace,

And so cast out demons and banish sickness,

That whatever it touches may be delivered from all wickedness,

And be set free from all danger,

So that no spirit of disease or immorality will remain.

From its presence let all demonic attacks against the safety and peace of believers, or anything that is theirs, flee,

So that the wellbeing which they seek through prayer in your name, may be theirs

Through Jesus Christ our Lord. * Amen.

The Mingling of Salt and Water

[The priest will sprinkle the salt in the water in the sign of the cross, and say . . .]

> Let this salt and water be mingled together in the name of
>
> The † Father,
>
> And of the † Son,
>
> And of the † Holy Spirit. * Amen.

The Blessing of the Mingled Elements

[Holding his hand over the mingled salt and water, the priest says . . .]

> Let us pray.
>
> Lord Jesus:
>
> You are God Almighty.
>
> You are the King of kings.
>
> You are the overwhelming conqueror over all your foes.
>
> You are the destroyer of everything which exalts itself against you.
>
> You are ruler of the stormy sea.
>
> You are the orderer of chaos.
>
> You are the terror of demon hoards.
>
> You are victorious over all evil.
>
> With awe, wonder, and confidence in your grace, we ask that you, O Lord, together with your Father and the Holy Spirit,
>
> Bless † this mixture of salt and water,

Sanctifying † it with your grace,

That wherever it is sprinkled with the name of the Holy Trinity,

All demonic presences * may be driven away,

All fear of evil spirits * may be driven away,

All disease of mind, body, or spirit * may be driven away,

And the presence of the Holy Spirit may be graciously given to all who ask for your mercy, through your name, who, together with your Father and Spirit, are to be worshipped and glorified unto the ages of ages. * Amen.

[Once blessed, the holy water should be kept in a safe, convenient location.] [1]

1. This appendix is from material adapted from *A Manual for Priests,* interviews with other priests, and personal notes.

Appendix C

Prayers of Deliverance

IN THE PRAYERS THAT follow, whenever † appears, the minister should make the sign of the cross over the victim or on his/her forehead. The minister is strongly encouraged to use holy water or holy oil to make the sign.

A Prayer for Deliverance against the Attacks of the Evil One

> Lord have mercy!
>
> † God, our Lord,
>
> † King of the ages,
>
> † All-powerful and Almighty,
>
> You who made everything and who transforms everything simply by your will;
>
> You who in Babylon changed the flames of the seven-times hotter furnace into refreshing coolness and protected and saved the three Hebrew children:
>
> You are the doctor and physician of our souls;
>
> You are the salvation of those who turn to you.
>
> We humbly ask you to make powerless, banish, and drive out every diabolic power, presence, and machination;

Every evil influence, curse, malediction, and all evil actions aimed against your servant _____.

Where there is envy and malice, give your servant an abundance of goodness, endurance, victory, and charity.

O Lord, you who love humankind,

We beg you to reach out your powerful hands and your most high and mighty arms and come to your servant's aid.

Help your servant, who is made in your image;

Send your holy angel of peace over him/her, to protect him/her body and soul.

Keep at bay and vanquish every evil power, every poison or malice invoked against him/her by corrupt and envious people.

Then, under the protection of your authority may he/she sing in gratitude: "The Lord is my salvation; whom should I fear?

"I will not fear, because you are with me, my God, my strength, my powerful Lord, Lord of peace, Father of all ages."

Yes! Lord our God—be merciful to your servant, your image,

And save him/her from every threat or harm from the evil one,

And protect him/her by raising him/her above all evil.

We ask you this through the intercessions of him who ever lives to make intercession for the saints, even Jesus Christ our Lord. Amen.[1]

---

1. Adapted from the Liturgy of Exorcism by St. John Chrysostom.

A Prayer for Sanctification

† Soul of Christ, sanctify your servant, _____.

† Body of Christ, save your servant.

† Blood of Christ, inebriate your servant.

† Water from the side of Christ, wash him/her.

† Passion of Christ, strengthen him/her.

O good Jesus, hear my prayer for your servant—

Within your wounds hide him/her.

Let him/her never be separate from you.

From the evil one, protect him/her.

At the hour of death, call him/her and bid him/her come to you that with your saints he/she may praise you forever. Amen.[2]

A Prayer Against Every Evil

God the †Father,

And God the †Son,

And God the †Holy Spirit,

God the Most Holy Trinity:

Descend upon this man (woman),

Purify him/her, Lord,

Shape him/her,

Fill him/her with yourself, and use him/her.

Banish all forces of evil from him/her, destroy them, vanquish them,

---

2. *Anima Christi,* traditional.

So that he/she may be healthy and do good deeds.

Banish from him/her all spells, witchcraft, black magic, evil works, ties, curses, maledictions,

Diabolic infections, oppressions, possessions;

All that is evil and sinful—jealousy, faithlessness, envy, physical, psychological, moral, spiritual, and diabolic ailments.

Burn all these evils in hell, that they may never again touch him/her or any other creature in the entire world.

I command and bid all powers who molest this child of God—

By the power of God the Father Almighty,

In the name of Jesus Christ our Savior,

And through the mighty work of the Holy Spirit—

To leave him/her forever,

And to be consigned into the everlasting hell,

Bound by the holy angels of God

And crushed beneath the heel of Jesus Christ. Amen.[3]

A Prayer for Spiritual Healing

Holy Jesus, you are the Great Physician who came into the world to heal the broken hearted.

We ask you to heal the suffering that causes fear in the mind and heart of your child.

We ask to heal and save all who have sinned against him/her.

We ask you to fill your child by your Holy Spirit and heal him/her of the physical, mental, emotional, and spiritual

---

3. Adapted from Amorth, *An Exorcist Tells his Story,* 199.

wounds that struck him/her during his/her childhood and from the resulting pain which afflicted him/her throughout his/her life.

Lord Jesus, you know how burdened your child is; by your Holy Spirit, cause him/her to cast them all upon you.

We ask you—by your grace—to heal his/her wounds. Heal his/her memories, so that nothing that has happened to him/her will continue to afflict him/her.

Heal all those wounds that have caused so much evil in his/her life.

Give him/her grace that he/she may forgive all those who have sinned against him/her.

Heal those wounds that make it difficult for him/her to forgive.

You who came to forgive, forgive him/her; you who came to heal, heal him/her; you who came to save, save him/her.

Heal him/her, O Lord, from any pain caused by the death of his/her loved ones.

Grant him/her peace and joy in the assurance that you are the Resurrection and the Life.

Make him/her an authentic witness to your resurrection, your victory over sin and death, your living presence among us, and your return for us. Amen.[4]

A Lesser Litany of Deliverance

[To be said by the minister with the victim responding (as indicated by R) together with others who may be present.]

Lord, you are all powerful,

4. Ibid, 203.

R: You are God, you are Father.

We beg you to send your holy warrior angels and all the hosts of heaven,

R: To deliver our brothers and sisters from slavery to the evil one.

From anxiety, sadness, and obsessions,

R: Free us, O Lord.

From hatred, fornication, and envy,

R: Free us, O Lord.

From thoughts of jealousy, rage, and death,

R: Free us, O Lord.

From every thought of suicide and abortion,

R: Free us, O Lord.

From every form of sinful sexuality,

R: Free us, O Lord.

From every division of family and every harmful friendship,

R: Free us, O Lord.

From every sort of spell, curse, witchcraft, and every form of the occult,

R: Free us, O Lord.

Lord, you who said, "I leave you peace, my peace I give you," grant that we may be liberated from every evil work and enjoy your peace always, in the name of Christ, our Lord. Amen.[5]

5. Traditional.

Appendix D

Renouncing Family Curses and Maledictions

General Instructions

The renouncing of family curses and maledictions should be done by the person under attack in front of at least two witnesses not of his or her family, though the additional presence of other members of his or her family is often beneficial. At least one of the witnesses should be a trained minister of deliverance. In the event of a curse or malediction directed against an entire family, the renunciation has its best effect when done by the head of the household. It may be helpful to burn or otherwise destroy some family object associated with the person(s) who is (are) associated with instigating or perpetuating the curse or malediction. Instructions are set off with brackets.

A Rite of Renunciation

I declare, in the name of God Almighty—

† [signs him or herself] The Father,

† The Son,

And † the Holy Spirit,

In the presence of his divine majesty,

The angelic hosts of heaven,

Satan and his demons,

And these witnesses,

That I renounce the sins of my ancestors and repent of my sinful responses to them.

By the mighty power of the Holy God, the Father, the Son, and the Holy Spirit,

I break all the curses brought on to me and my family by these sins—

Whether by rite or ceremony, by word spoken against them or me.

I renounce this diabolic heritage

And in Jesus' name declare myself, my family, and my descendants to be disinherited from these curses and maledictions from this day forward.

I reject the consequences of this heritage,

Whether physical, emotional, psychological, or spiritual;

Whether regarding me, my family, or my descendants;

Or regarding our godly prosperity, including property and possessions.

I renounce and break, for myself and my family,

All ungodly covenants, agreements, contracts, oaths, promises, pacts, blood oaths, and soul ties.

I renounce the sins which made and bound these covenants

And all sins which are consequences thereof.

I renounce all occult practices, societies, and their spirits, specifically . . . [they are named]

I renounce all forms of heresy and false religion, specifically . . .

I renounce diseases of mind, body, emotion, or spirit, specifically . . .

I renounce addictions to substances and behaviors, specifically . . .

I renounce the illicit use of God's gifts, specifically . . .

This is my solemn covenant which I make before God, heaven, hell, and these witnesses

In the name of Jesus Christ, his Holy Father, and life-giving Spirit. Amen.[1]

---

1. Adapted from multiple sources, including interviews with clergy and personal notes.

Appendix E

A Rite for House Cleansing and Blessing

General Instructions

Performing the house cleansing rite should involve as much of the family as is reasonable, taking into account the family members's ages, maturity, spiritual condition, willingness to participate, and health. It is also a good idea to have a team involved that includes at least one person with the gift of discerning of spirits. The priest should have on a purple stole, a surplice (optional), and a good supply of holy water. The priest says the liturgy, the others present responding. When a cross (†) appears in the text, the priest makes the sign of the cross over those indicated with holy water. Instructions are indicated by brackets. An R indicates responses by others present.

The Rite

Invocation

> The Lord be with you.
>
> R: And also with you.

A Rite for House Cleansing and Blessing

Let us pray.

Come, O Father, into this home, and be its head, its shield and defense,

Be present here with your grace,

Be known here by your love,

Be merciful in your grace to those who dwell here;

Through Jesus Christ our Lord, who with you and the Holy Spirit lives and reigns, one God, forever and ever.

R: Amen.

The Binding Prayer

In the name of God the Father, and in the name of Jesus Christ, his only Son our Lord, and by the power of the Holy Spirit,

We † [priest sprinkles the room] bind and cast out all evil spirits in all the elements,

Here, above, and below,

In the spirit realm and the natural.

We † bind and break all curses, hexes, spells, maledictions, hauntings, witchcraft, or occult activity.

We bind and break all demonic alliances.

And we claim the protection of the shed blood of Jesus Christ

Over this house and grounds, and every person here.

We call upon you, O Holy Spirit: sanctify this dwelling and fill it with your presence.

We call upon you, O Jesus: cover and undergird this house with your grace.

We call upon you, O Father: send your angels to guard this home, set aside by prayer to be holy.

We call upon you, Most Holy and Glorious Trinity: come, fill this place, and never leave!

R: Amen.

Prayer of Blessing

The Lord be with you.

R: And also with you.

Let us pray.

Father, thank you that you have called this family and filled them with the holy desire that all they are, all they do, and all they possess be dedicated wholly to you, together with your Son and Holy Spirit.

Bless this home, and all who dwell herein. May it be for them a refuge of peace, comfort, and joy.

May the gift of hospitality be evident to all. May this family be blessed to be a blessing; kept in health to bring healing; be joyful to impart joy; live as kingdom servants to serve others; and live at peace that they may be peacemakers.

Strengthen them in their resolve to serve you and live as faithful witnesses of your love and grace.

Father, † [priest sprinkles the family] bless and sanctify them, and enrich them according to your grace that they may prosper in all ways. Pour upon them, O Lord, the continual fountain of your heavenly blessings.

Hear their prayers which they offer in this place—may they never be hindered. Answer their prayers in accordance your great love and mercy. Empower their prayers that this home may be a haven of blessing and peace.

Lord, bless this home—in every part. Clean it from every past evil; cause it to be a holy sanctuary; may it be a beacon of your love and a fountain of your blessings; may it be a place where your holy angels are known to reside and to stand watch over all those who dwell herein; through Jesus Christ our Lord.

R: Amen.

For Each Room

Arise, O Lord, Holy God, the † [priest sprinkles the room] Father, the † Son, and the † Holy Spirit. Banish from this place every unclean spirit and protect those who live here from every evil.

R: Amen.

Prayers for Each Room

[It is a good practice to say an extemporaneous prayer appropriate for each room, such as binding and banishing the spirit of accidents in bathrooms, kitchens, and on the stairs; and the spirit of marital discord in the bedroom.]

Response to Evil Presences

[If there is a place where an evil presence is detected, then proclaim in a loud and confident voice the words of Ps. 68:1. Repeat until the presence has fled.]

†Let God arise! †Let His enemies be scattered! †Let those who hate Him flee before Him!

Benediction

May the Lord bless you and keep you; may the Lord make his face to shine upon you and be gracious unto you; may the Lord lift up the light of his countenance upon you and give you peace, this day and evermore—in the name of †the Father, the Son, and the Holy Spirit.

R: Amen.

Appendix F

Informed Consent and Confidentiality Agreement

I, _____, (I, _____, parent or guardian of _____), have read, understood, and consent to the following provisions:

1. All of my/my child's/my ward's personal information will remain confidential except as provided below.

2. I give permission for _____ (hereafter known as the minister) to perform rites, offer prayers, and counsel.

3. I give permission to the minister to inform my/my child's/my ward's pastor, _____. Specifically, the minister may inform the pastor of the following: _____

_____

_____

_____

_____

_____.

4. I give permission to the minister, my/my child's/my ward's physician (_____), and my/my child's/my ward's mental health professional (_____) to exchange information and consult with each other on matters related to the deliverance ministry.

5. I give permission to the minister to consult with other ministers provided that my/my child's/my ward's personal information remains confidential.

6. I or the minister have the right to cease involvement in the deliverance ministry, whether temporarily or permanently.

7. All matters will be handled in accordance with the Scriptures and the doctrinal, canonical, and sacramental norms of the Anglican Church in North America.

8. I have the right to an explanation for any and all aspects of the deliverance ministry.

_____

Printed Name

_____

Signature

_____

Date

Witness A:

_____

Printed Name

_____

Signature

_____

Date

INFORMED CONSENT AND CONFIDENTIALITY AGREEMENT

Witness B:

_____

Printed Name

_____

Signature

_____

Date

Minister(s)

Printed name(s) of minister(s)

_____

_____

_____

_____

I/we, the above named minister(s), have read, understood, and consent to the following provisions:

1. All personal information will remain confidential except as provided above.

2. Rites, prayers, and counseling will only be offered with consent as provided above.

3. All parties have the right to cease involvement in the deliverance ministry, whether temporarily or permanently.

4. All matters will be handled in accordance with the Scriptures and the doctrinal, canonical, and sacramental norms of the Anglican Church in North America.

_____

Signature

_____

Date

_____

Signature

_____

Date

_____

Signature

_____

Date

_____

Signature

_____

Date

Appendix G

Exorcism Rites

First Rite (Based on the Exorcism Rite of St. Basil the Great)

General Instructions

The minister, together with any other clergy, should wear a surplice and a purple stole. The rite should be preceded by the service of holy communion at which all the deliverance team communes. Care should be taken as to whether the victim should participate in the sacrament. During each prayer of exorcism, the minister may lay an end of his stole around the neck of the victim. The rite begins with the Litany from the Book of Common Prayer. At any time during the rite, if so moved by the Holy Spirit, the minister may make other prayers to God and commands to the demons. Responses by other participants are indicated by R. To avoid confusion, instructions are set off by brackets. Unless otherwise stated, † indicates that the minister should make the sign of the cross over the victim using holy water.

A Reading from the Psalter

[The assisting minister reads the following.]

The Lord be with you.

R: And also with you.

Let us read Psalm 53 responsively by whole verse.

> ¹ The fool says in his heart, "There is no God." They are corrupt, doing abominable iniquity; there is none who does good.
>
> ² God looks down from heaven on the children of man to see if there are any who understand, who seek after God.
>
> ³ They have all fallen away; together they have become corrupt; there is none who does good, not even one.
>
> ⁴ Have those who work evil no knowledge, who eat up my people as they eat bread, and do not call upon God?
>
> ⁵ There they are, in great terror, where there is no terror! For God scatters the bones of him who encamps against you; you put them to shame, for God has rejected them.
>
> ⁶ Oh, that salvation for Israel would come out of Zion! When God restores the fortunes of his people, let Jacob rejoice, let Israel be glad.
>
> Glory be to the Father, and to the Son, and to the Holy Spirit.

R: As it was in the beginning, is now and ever shall be, world without end. Amen.

The Command

[The command which follows should be said forcefully and confidently by the exorcist. If at any time the spirits should reveal themselves, the minister should say: "Come out, unclean spirit _____ in the name of Jesus Christ. I bind you and command you do depart into Hell and there await your judgment!"]

I command you, O unclean spirits,

In the name † of the Father,

And † of the Son,

And † of the Holy Spirit,

That you harm no one here present,

That you harm not one of the families of those here present,

That you harm none of the possessions or positions of life of those here present.

I command you, O unclean spirits,

In the name † the Father Almighty,

And † of Jesus Christ, his only Son our Lord,

And † of the Holy Spirit, who with the Father and the Son is together one God,

That you make no display to invoke fear, laughter, confusion, or distraction;

That you do not speak unless I command you,

And then only to say what I bid you to say.

I command you, O unclean spirits,

In name of the † Holy and † most glorious † Trinity,

In the name of the Father, whose son/daughter this is,

In the name of Jesus Christ, who saved his/her soul,

In the name of the Holy Spirit, who raised Christ from the dead

And who will raise his/her mortal body at the day of resurrection,

That you reveal all of your names,

That none of you hide yourselves by any deception,

And that you obey all of the commands which I,

As a minister of the glorious Gospel of Jesus Christ,

Shall give you.

Name yourselves now! [Pause]

The First Prayer

Let us pray to the Lord.

R: Lord, have mercy.

O God of gods and Lord of lords,

Creator of the fiery spirits and artificer of the invisible powers,

Of all things heavenly and earthly:

You who no man has seen—nor is able to see;

You whom all creation fears and before whom it trembles;

You who cast into the darkness of the abyss of Tartarus the angels who fell away with him who once was commander of the angelic host, who disobeyed you and haughtily refused to serve you:

Expel by the terror of your name the evil one and his legions loose upon the earth,

Lucifer and those with him who fell from above.

Set him to flight and command him and his demons to depart completely.

Let no harm come to them who are sealed in your image

And let those who are sealed receive dominion,

To tread on serpents and scorpions and all the power of the enemy.

For you do we exalt and praise

And with every breath do we glorify your all-holy name

Of the † Father,

And of the † Son,

And of the † Holy Spirit,

Now and ever and unto ages of ages.

R: Amen.

The Gospel Reading

[To be read by an assisting clergy (in the Anglican tradition this would be a deacon or priest). At †, cross successively the forehead, the mouth, and the heart. One or more of the following Gospel texts is read: John 1:1-14; Mark 16:15-18; Luke 10:17-20; 11:14-22.]

The † holy † Gospel according to † St. _____.

R: Glory be to you, O Lord.

[The reading being finished.]

The Gospel of the Lord.

R: Praise be to you, O Christ.

The Second Prayer

Let us pray to the Lord.

R: Lord, have mercy.

[The minister extends his hand toward the victim.]

I expel you and your servants,

Primal source of blasphemy,

Prince of the rebel host,

Originator of evil.

I expel you, Lucifer, together with all demons,

Who were cast from the brilliance on high

Into the darkness of the abyss on account of your arrogance:

I expel you and all the fallen hosts which followed your will.

I expel you, spirit(s) of uncleanness, known by the name(s) of _____, and unknown to us, who revolted against Adonai, Elohim,

The omnipotent God of Sabaoth and the army of his angels.

Be gone and depart from the servant/handmaid of God [say the victim's name].

I expel you in the name of him

Who created all things by his Word,

His only-begotten † Son, our Lord Jesus Christ,

Who was ineffably and dispassionately born before all the ages;

By whom was formed all things visible and invisible,

Who made man after his image,

Who guarded man by the angels,

Who trained him in the Law,

Who drowned sin in the flood of waters from above

And who shut up the abysses under the heaven,

Who demolished the impious race of giants,

Who shook down the tower of Babel,

Who reduced Sodom and Gomorrah to ashes by sulfur and fire,

And who by the staff of Moses separated the waters of the Red Sea, opening a waterless path for the people, while the tyrannical Pharaoh and his God-fighting army were drowned forever in its waves for his wicked persecution of them,

And who in these last days was inexplicably incarnate of the Blessed Virgin Mary, the Theotokos[1]

And who was pleased to purge our ancient defilement in the baptismal cleansing.

I expel you, Satan,

By virtue of Christ's baptism in the Jordan, which for us is a type of our inheritance of incorruption through grace and sanctified waters:

The same one who astounded the angels and all the heavenly powers when they beheld God incarnate in the flesh and also revealed at the Jordan his beginningless † Father and the † Holy Spirit with whom he shares the unity of the † Trinity.

I expel you, evil one,

In the name of him who rebuked the winds and stilled the turbulent sea;

Who banished the legion of demons,

---

1. Many of the ancient exorcism rituals ask for the intercession of Mary and the saints. This is contrary to the practices of the reformed catholicism of Anglicanism. However, the mention of Mary and the saints is a reminder that we surrounded by a great cloud of witnesses (Heb 12:1). Additionally, mention of Mary as the *Theotokos* (God-bearer), as prescribed by the Third and Fourth Councils, is a reminder of Christ's true incarnation, which doctrine the heretics and demon-possessed deny and the demons greatly revile and fear (1 John 4:1-6).

And opened the eyes of him who was born blind from his mother's womb;

And who from clay fashioned sight for the blind man, whereby he re-enacted the ancient refashioning of our face;

Who restored the speech of the speechless, purged the stigma of leprosy, raised the dead from the grave,

And who himself despoiled Hades by his death and resurrection thereby rendering mankind impervious to death.

I expel you, in the name of almighty God

Who filled men with the inbreathing of a divinely in-spired voice and who wrought, together with the Apos-tles, the piety which has filled the universe.

Fear and flee, run, leave, unclean and accursed spirit, deceitful and unseemly creature of the infernal depths,

Visible through deceit, hidden by pretense.

Depart wherever you may appear, Beelzebub,

Vanish as smoke and heat, bestial and serpentine thing;

Whether disguised as male or female;

Whether beast or crawling thing or flying;

Whether garrulous, mute, or speechless,

Whether bringing fear of being trampled, or rending apart, conniving;

Whether oppressing him/her in sleep, by some display of weakness, by distracting laughter, or taking pleasure in false tears;

Whether by lechery or stench of carnal lust, pleasure, ad-diction to drugs, divination or astrology;

Whether dwelling in a house;

Whether possessed by audacity, or contentiousness, or instability;

Whether striking him with lunacy or returning to him after the passage of time;

Whether you be of the morning, noonday, midnight or night, indefinite time, or daybreak;

Whether spontaneously, or sent to someone, or coming upon him/her unawares;

Whether from the sea, a river, from beneath the earth, from a well, a ravine, a hollow, a lake, a thicket of reeds, from matter, land, or refuse;

Whether from a grove, a tree, a thicket, from a fowl, or thunder;

Whether from the precincts of a bath, a pool of water, or from a pagan sepulcher, or from any place where you may lurk;

Whether by knowledge, ignorance, or any place not mentioned.

Depart, separate yourself from him/her;

Be ashamed before him/her who was made in the image of God and shaped by his hand.

Fear the likeness of the incarnate God and no longer hide in his servant/handmaid_____;

Rather await the rod of iron, the fiery furnace of Tartarus, and the gnashing of teeth as reprisal for disobedience.

Be afraid, be still, flee, neither return nor hide in him/her some other kind of evil, unclean spirits.

Depart into the uncultivated, waterless waste of the desert where no man dwells, where God alone vigilantly watches,

Who shall bind you that dares with envy to plot against his image,

And who, with chains of darkness, shall hold you in Tartarus,

Who by day, and night, and for a great length of time, has devised all manner of torment, O devil;

For great is your fear of God,

And great is the glory of the † Father, of the † Son, and of the Holy † Spirit.

R: Amen.

Scripture Lesson

[An assisting minister reads one or more of the following lessons: Rev 20:1-15; 2 Cor 10:3-6; 1 Peter 5:6-11; Eph 6:10-18.]

A reading from _____.

[The scripture being read.]

The Word of the Lord.

R: Thanks be to God.

The Third Prayer

[The minister makes the sign of the cross over himself and the one possessed, places the end of the stole on the latter's neck (if he is not already doing so), and places his right hand on the latter's head, saying the third prayer forcefully and confidently. At † the minister makes the sign of the cross on the forehead of the victim with holy oil.]

Let us pray to the Lord.

R: Lord, have mercy.

O God of the heavens,

God of light,

God of the angels and archangels obedient to your authority and power;

O God who is glorified in your saints,

† Father of our Lord Jesus Christ, your only-begotten Son, who delivered the souls which were bound to death and who enlightened them that dwelt in darkness;

Who released us from all our misery and pain and who has protected us from the assaults of the enemy;

And † you, O Son and Word of God,

Who has purposed us for immortality by your death and glorified us with your glory;

You who loosed us from the fetters of our sins through your cross, rendering us pleasing to yourself and uniting us with God;

You who rescued us from destruction and cured all our diseases;

You who set us on the path to heaven and changed our corruption to incorruption:

Hear me as I call unto you with longing and awe;

You before whom the mountains and the firmament under the heavens do shrink;

You who make the physical elements tremble, keeping them within their own limits;

And because of whom the fires of retribution dare not overstep the boundary set for them but must await the decision of your will;

And for whom all creation sighs with great sighs awaiting deliverance;

By whom all adverse natures have been put to flight and the legion of the enemy has been subdued, the devil is made afraid, the serpent trampled underfoot, and the dragon slain;

You who have enlightened the nations which confess and welcome your rule, O Lord;

You through whom life has appeared, hope has prevailed;

Through whom the man of the earth was recreated by belief in you.

For who is like unto you, almighty God?

Wherefore we beseech you, O † Father,

Lord of mercies,

Who existed before the ages and surpasses all good,

Calling upon your holy name, through the love of your child, † Jesus Christ, the holy one, and your all-powerful † Spirit:

Cast away from _____'s soul every malady and all disbelief;

Spare him/her from the furious attacks of unclean, infernal, fiery, evil-serving, lustful spirits, the love of gold and silver, conceit, fornication, every shameless, unseemly, dark and profane demon.

Indeed, O God, expel from your servant/handmaiden _____ every energy of the devil, every enchantment and delusion; all idolatry, lunacy, astrology, necromancy, every superstition;

The love of luxury and the flesh, all greed, drunkenness, carnality, adultery, licentiousness, shamelessness, anger, contentiousness, confusion, and all evil suspicion.

Yes! O Lord our God,

Breathe upon him/her the Spirit of your peace;

Watch over him/her and produce thereby the fruits of faith, virtue, wisdom, chastity, self-control, love, uprightness, hope, meekness, longsuffering, patience, prudence, and understanding in your servant/handmaiden;

That he/she may be welcomed by you in the name of Jesus Christ, believing in the coessential Trinity, giving witness and glorifying your dominion, along with the angels and archangels and all the heavenly host, guarding our hearts by them; for all things are possible to you, O Lord.

Therefore, we ascribe glory to the † Father, and to the † Son, and to the † Holy Spirit, now and ever and unto the ages of ages.

R: Amen.

[The above may be repeated as often as necessary. If the minister senses in the spirit that the time has come to end the exorcism, either because it has achieved its end, or because there is a need to resume the exorcism at another time, then the service concludes with the following:]

A Canticle

[Either the *Magnificat* (Luke 1:46-55) or the *Benedictus est* (Luke 1:68-79), followed by the Gloria, is read responsively by whole verse, the assistant leading.]

Prayer Following Deliverance

Almighty God, we beg you to keep the evil spirit(s), known by the name(s) of _____ or unknown to us, from further molesting this servant of yours, and to keep him/them far away, never to return.

At your command, O Lord, may the goodness and peace of our Lord Jesus Christ, our redeemer, take possession of this man (woman).

May we no longer fear any evil since the Lord is with us; who lives and reigns with you, in the unity of the Holy Spirit, one God, forever and ever.

R: Amen.

The Blessing

[The minister sprinkles the victim with holy water and says the following blessing:]

> May the peace of God, which passes all understanding keep your heart and mind in the knowledge and love of God and of his Son, Jesus Christ our Lord;
>
> And may the blessing of almighty God, † the Father, † the Son, and † the Holy Spirit,
>
> Be upon you and remain with you forever.
>
> R: Amen.

Second Rite (Based on the Exorcism Rite of St. John Chrysostom)

General Instructions

The minister, together with any other clergy, should wear a surplice and a purple stole. The rite should be preceded by the service of holy communion at which all the deliverance team communes. Care should be taken as to whether the victim should participate in the sacrament. During each prayer of exorcism, the minister may lay an end of his stole around the neck of the victim. The rite begins with the Litany from the Book of Common Prayer. At any time during the rite, if so moved by the Holy Spirit, the minister may make other prayers to God and commands to the demons. Responses by other participants are indicated by R. To avoid confusion, instructions are set off by brackets. Unless otherwise stated, † indicates that the minister should make the sign of the cross over the victim using holy water.

A Reading from the Psalter

[The assisting minister reads the following.]

The Lord be with you.

R: And also with you.

Let us read Psalm 53 responsively by whole verse.

[1] The fool says in his heart, "There is no God." They are corrupt, doing abominable iniquity; there is none who does good.

[2] God looks down from heaven on the children of man to see if there are any who understand, who seek after God.

[3] They have all fallen away; together they have become corrupt; there is none who does good, not even one.

[4] Have those who work evil no knowledge, who eat up my people as they eat bread, and do not call upon God?

[5] There they are, in great terror, where there is no terror! For God scatters the bones of him who encamps against you; you put them to shame, for God has rejected them.

[6] Oh, that salvation for Israel would come out of Zion! When God restores the fortunes of his people, let Jacob rejoice, let Israel be glad.

Glory be to the Father, and to the Son, and to the Holy Spirit.

R: As it was in the beginning, is now and ever shall be, world without end. Amen.

The Command

[The command which follows should be said forcefully and confidently. If at any time the spirits should reveal themselves, the minister should say: "Come out, unclean spirit _____ in the name of Jesus Christ. I bind you and command you do depart into Hell and there await your judgment!"]

I command you, O unclean spirits,

In the name † of the Father,

And † of the Son,

And † of the Holy Spirit,

That you harm no one here present,

That you harm not one of the families of those here present,

That you harm none of the possessions or positions of life of those here present.

I command you, O unclean spirits,

In the name † the Father almighty,

And † of Jesus Christ, his only Son our Lord,

And † of the Holy Spirit, who with the Father and the Son is together one God,

That you make no display to invoke fear, or laughter, or confusion, or distraction;

That you do not speak unless I command you, and then only to say what I bid you to say.

I command you, O unclean spirits,

In name of the † holy and † most glorious † Trinity,

In the name of the Father, whose son/daughter this is,

In the name of Jesus Christ, who saved his/her soul,

In the name of the Holy Spirit, who raised Christ from the dead and who will raise his/her mortal body at the day of resurrection,

That you reveal all of your names,

That none of you hide yourselves by any deception,

And that you obey all of the commands which I, as a minister of the glorious Gospel of Jesus Christ, shall give you.

Name yourselves now! [Pause]

The First Prayer

Let us pray to the Lord.

R: Lord, have mercy.

O eternal God,

Who has redeemed the race of men from the captivity of the devil,

Deliver your servant/handmaid _____

From all the workings of unclean spirits.

Command the evil and impure spirits and demons, both known to us by the name(s) of _____ or unknown to us,

To depart from the soul and body of your servant/handmaid and not to remain nor hide in him/her.

Let them be banished from this the creation of your hands in your own † holy name and that of your only-begotten † Son and of your life-creating † Spirit,

So that, after being cleansed from all demonic influence,

He/she may live godly, justly and righteously and may be counted worthy to receive the Holy mysteries of your only-begotten Son and our God,

With whom you are blessed and glorified together with the all holy and good and life-creating Spirit now and ever and unto the ages of ages.

R: Amen.

Appendix G

Gospel Reading

[One or more of the following Gospel texts is read by an assisting clergy: John 1:1-14; Mark 16:15-18; Luke 10:17-20; 11:14-22. At †, cross successively the forehead, the mouth, and the heart.]

The † holy Gospel according to St. . . .

R: Glory be to you, O Lord.

[The reading being finished]

The Gospel of the Lord.

R: Praise be to you, O Christ.

The Second Prayer

Let us pray to the Lord.

R: Lord, have mercy.

[The minister extends his hand toward the victim.]

O you who rebuked all unclean spirits and by the power of your Word has banished the legion,

Come now, through your only-begotten Son upon this creature, which you have fashioned in your own image,

And deliver him/her from the adversary(ies) that hold(s) him/her in bondage;

So that, receiving your mercy and becoming purified,

He/she might join the ranks of your holy flock,

And be preserved as a living temple of the Holy Spirit,

And might receive the divine and holy mysteries,

Through the grace and compassion and loving kindness of your only-begotten † Son with whom † you are blessed,

94

Together with your all-holy and good and life-creating
† Spirit,

Now and ever and unto the ages of ages.

R: Amen.

Scripture Lesson

A reading from _____

[An assisting minister reads one or more of the following lessons:
Rev 20:1-15; 2 Cor 10:3-6; 1 Peter 5:6-11; Eph 6:10-18.]

[The reading being finished]

The Word of the Lord.

R: Thanks be to God.

The Third Prayer

[At † the minister makes the sign of the cross on the forehead of
the victim with holy oil.]

Let us pray to the Lord.

R: Lord, have mercy.

We call upon you, O Lord,

Almighty God, Most High, untempted, peaceful king.

We call upon you who created the heaven and the earth,

For out of you has issued the Alpha and the Omega, the
beginning and the end;

You who have ordained that the four-footed and irrational
beasts be under subjection to man, for you have
subjected them.

Lord, stretch out your mighty hand and your sublime and holy arm,

And in your watchful care look down upon this † your creature

And send down upon him/her a peaceful angel, a mighty angel, a guardian of soul and body,

That will rebuke and drive away every evil and unclean demon from him/her;

For you alone are Lord, most high, almighty and blessed unto ages of ages.

R: Amen.

The Fourth Prayer (the Great Exorcism)

[The minister makes the sign of the cross over himself and the one possessed, places the end of the stole on the latter's neck (if he is not already doing so), and places his right hand on the latter's head, saying the Fourth Prayer forcefully and confidently. At † the minister makes the sign of the cross on the forehead of the victim with holy oil.]

Let us pray to the Lord.

R: Lord, have mercy.

We make this great, divine, holy, and awesome invocation, O devil, for your expulsion,

As well as this rebuke for your utter annihilation, O apostate one!

God who is holy, beginningless, frightful, invisible in essence,

Infinite in power and incomprehensible in divinity,

The king of glory and Lord almighty:

He shall rebuke you, devil!

Exorcism Rites

He who has composed all things well by his Word from nothingness into being;

He who walks upon the wings of the air:

The Lord rebukes you, devil!

He who calls forth the water of the sea and pours it upon the face of all the earth;

Lord of hosts is his name:

Devil, the Lord rebukes you!

He who is ministered to and praised by numberless heavenly orders and adored and glorified in fear by multitudes of angelic and archangelic hosts:

Satan, the Lord rebukes you!

He who is honored by the encircling powers,

The awesome six-winged and many-eyed cherubim and seraphim that cover their faces with two wings because of his inscrutable and unseen divinity, and with two wings cover their feet, lest they be seared by his unutterable glory and incomprehensible majesty, and with two wings do fly and fill the heavens with their shouts of "Holy, holy, holy, Lord sabaoth, heaven and earth are full of your glory!":

Devil, the Lord rebukes you!

He who came down from the Father's bosom and, through the holy, inexpressible, immaculate and adorable incarnation from the Virgin,

Appeared ineffably in the world to save it and cast you down from heaven in his authoritative power and showed you to be an outcast to every man:

Satan, the Lord rebukes you!

He who said to the sea, be silent, be still, and instantly it was calmed at his command:

Devil, the Lord rebukes you!

He who made clay with his immaculate spittle and re-fashioned the withered eye of the man blind from birth and gave him his sight:

Devil, the Lord rebukes you!

He who by his word restored to life the daughter of the ruler of the synagogue, and snatched the son of the widow out from the mouth of death and gave him whole and sound to his own mother:

Devil, the Lord rebukes you!

The Lord who raised Lazarus the four-days dead from the dead, un-decayed, as if not having died, and unblemished to the astonishment of many:

Satan, the Lord rebukes you!

He who destroyed the curse by the blow on his face,

And by the lance in his immaculate side,

Lifted the flaming sword that guarded Paradise:

Devil, the Lord rebukes you!

He who dried all tears from every face by the spitting upon His precious expressed image:

Devil, the Lord rebukes you!

He who set his cross as a support,

The salvation of the world,

To your fall and the fall of all the angels under you:

Devil, the Lord rebukes you!

He who spoke from his cross

And the curtain of the temple was torn in two,

The rocks were split,

The tombs were opened,

And those who were dead from the ages were raised up:

EXORCISM RITES

Devil, the Lord rebukes you!

He who by death put death to death and by his rising granted life to all men:

May the Lord rebuke you, Satan!

The Lord who descended into Hades and opened its tombs

And set free those held prisoner in it, calling them to himself;

Before whom the gatekeepers of Hades shuddered when they saw him and, hiding themselves, vanished in the anguish of Hades:

May the Lord rebuke you, devil!

The Lord, Christ our God,

Who arose from the dead and granted his resurrection to all men:

May the Lord rebuke you, Satan!

He who in glory ascended into heaven to his Father,

And sits on the right of majesty upon the throne of glory:

Devil, may the Lord rebuke you!

He who shall come again with glory upon the clouds of heaven with his holy angels to judge the living and the dead:

Devil, may the Lord rebuke you!

He who has prepared for you unquenchable fire,

The unsleeping worm,

And the outer darkness unto eternal punishment:

Devil, may the Lord rebuke you!

For before him all things shudder and tremble

And from the face of his power and the wrath of his doom upon you is uncontainable.

Satan, the Lord rebukes you by his frightful name!

Shudder, tremble, be afraid, depart, be utterly destroyed, be banished!

You who fell from heaven and together with you all evil spirits, including the spirit(s) known to us by the name(s) of _____ and those unknown to us:

Every evil spirit of lust, the spirit of evil;

A day and nocturnal spirit, a noonday and evening spirit, a midnight spirit;

An imaginative spirit, an encountering spirit, either of the dry land or of the water, or one in a forest, or among the reeds, or in trenches, or in a road or a crossroad, in lakes, or streams;

In houses, or one sprinkling in the baths and chambers, or one altering the mind of man.

The Lord rebuke you! Even the Lord God of Israel!

Depart swiftly from this creature of the creator Christ our God!

And be gone from the † servant/handmaid of God _____;

From † his/her mind, from his/her soul;

From † his/her heart, from his/her will;

From † his/her senses, from all his/her members;

That he/she might become whole and sound and free, knowing God, his/her own master and creator of all things:

He who gathers together those who have gone astray

And who gives them the seal of salvation

Through the rebirth and restoration of divine baptism,

So that he may be counted worthy of his immaculate, heavenly and awesome mysteries and be united to his true fold,

Dwelling in a place of pasture and nourished on the waters of repose,

Guided pastorally and safely by the staff of the cross unto the forgiveness of sins and life everlasting.

For unto † him belongs all glory, honor, adoration and majesty,

Together with his beginningless † Father

And his all-holy, good and life-giving † Spirit,

Now and ever, and unto ages of ages.

R: Amen.

[The above may be repeated as often as necessary. If the minister senses in his spirit that the time has come to end the exorcism, either because it has achieved its end, or because there is a need to resume the exorcism at another time, then the service concludes with the following.]

A Canticle

[Either the *Magnificat* (Luke 1:46-55) or the *Benedictus est* (Luke 1:68-79), followed by the Gloria, is read responsively by whole verse, the assistant leading.]

Prayer Following Deliverance

Almighty God,

We beg you to keep the evil spirit(s), known to us by the name(s) of _____ and unknown to us, from further molesting this servant of yours, and to keep him/them far away, never to return.

At your command, O Lord, may the goodness and peace of our Lord Jesus Christ, our redeemer, take possession of this man (woman).

May we no longer fear any evil since the Lord is with us; who lives and reigns with you, in the unity of the Holy Spirit, God, forever and ever.

R: Amen.

The Blessing

[The minister sprinkles the victim with holy water and says the following blessing.]

May the peace of God, which passes all understanding, keep your heart and mind in the knowledge and love of God and of his Son, Jesus Christ our Lord.

And may the blessing of almighty God, † The Father, † the Son, and † the Holy Spirit,

Be upon you and remain with you forever.

R: Amen.

General Outline for Exorcism

General Instructions

For use by experienced ministers who wish to follow a generalized outline rather than a specific liturgy. Precede the rite with holy communion for all the members of the deliverance team. Exercise care as to whether or not you include the victim.

1. The Litany.

2. A reading from the Psalms.

3. A commandment to the evil spirits on how they are to obey during the exorcism and to reveal their names.

4. A prayer extolling God's character and saving actions.

5. An appropriate Scripture reading.

6. An imprecation in which the evil spirits are reminded that they are defeated.

7. An appropriate Scripture reading.

8. A prayer asking God to expel the wicked spirits followed by a command to the spirits to leave the victim.

9. A Scripture song of praise.

10. A prayer of thanksgiving for deliverance.

11. A benediction over the victim and the team.

Athanasian Creed

[A good test to see if the spirits have departed is to have the victim, together with all present, say responsively the following creed.]

> Whoever wills to be saved must before all else hold fast to the catholic faith.
>
> Unless one keeps this faith whole and untarnished, without doubt he will perish forever.
>
> Now this is the catholic faith: that we worship one God in Trinity, and Trinity in unity;
>
> Neither confusing the persons one with the other, nor making a distinction in their nature.
>
> For the Father is a distinct person; and so is the Son; and so is the Holy Spirit.
>
> Yet the Father, Son, and Holy Spirit possess one Godhead, co-equal glory, co-eternal majesty.
>
> As the Father is, so is the Son, so also is the Holy Spirit.
>
> The Father is uncreated, the Son is uncreated, the Holy Spirit is uncreated.

The Father is infinite, the Son is infinite, the Holy Spirit is infinite.

The Father is eternal, the Son is eternal, the Holy Spirit is eternal.

Yet they are not three eternals, but one eternal God;

Even as they are not three uncreated, or three infinites, but one uncreated and one infinite God.

So likewise the Father is almighty, the Son is almighty, the Holy Spirit is almighty.

Yet they are not three almighties, but they are the one Almighty.

Thus the Father is God, the Son is God, the Holy Spirit is God.

Yet they are not three gods, but one God.

Thus the Father is Lord, the Son is Lord, the Holy Spirit is Lord.

Yet there are not three lords, but one Lord.

For just as Christian truth compels us to profess that each person is individually God and Lord, so does the catholic religion forbid us to hold that there are three gods or lords.

The Father was not made by any power; he was neither created nor begotten.

The Son is from the Father alone, neither created nor made, but begotten.

The Holy Spirit is from the Father and the Son, neither made nor created nor begotten, but he proceeds.

So there is one Father, not three; one Son, not three; one Holy Spirit, not three.

And in this Trinity one person is not earlier or later, nor is one greater or less; but all three persons are co-eternal and co-equal.

In every way, then, as already affirmed, unity in Trinity and Trinity in unity is to be worshiped.

Whoever, then, wills to be saved must assent to this doctrine of the blessed Trinity.

But it is necessary for everlasting salvation that one also firmly believe in the incarnation of our Lord Jesus Christ.

True faith, then, requires us to believe and profess that our Lord Jesus Christ, the Son of God, is both God and man.

He is God, begotten of the substance of the Father from eternity; he is man, born in time of the substance of his mother.

He is perfect God, and perfect man subsisting in a rational soul and a human body.

He is equal to the Father in his divine nature, but less than the Father in his human nature as such.

And though he is God and man, yet he is the one Christ, not two;

One, however, not by any change of divinity into flesh, but by the act of God assuming a human nature.

He is one only, not by a mixture of substance, but by the oneness of his person.

For, somewhat as the rational soul and the body compose one man, so Christ is one person who is both God and man;

Who suffered for our salvation, who descended into hell, who rose again the third day from the dead;

Who ascended into heaven, and sits at the right hand of God the Father almighty, from there he shall come to judge both the living and the dead.

At his coming all men shall rise again in their bodies, and shall give an account of their works.

And those who have done good shall enter into everlasting life, but those who have done evil into everlasting fire.

All this is the catholic faith, and unless one believes it truly and firmly one cannot be saved.

Glory be to the Father, and to the Son, and to the Holy Spirit.

As it was in the beginning is now and ever shall be, world without end. Amen.

Appendix H

The Nature and Activities of Satan and Demons

Introduction

THE BIBLE DOES NOT speak as clearly on the matter of evil spirits and their actions as perhaps we would like. With very few exceptions, information about these entities is conveyed in the form of a narrative, and it is sometimes difficult to distinguish the merely descriptive from the didactic in these accounts. That said, let us attempt to construct a Biblical worldview regarding the diabolic realm and its subjects.

Satan

If we take the witness of the Scriptures seriously, we must believe that there is a being called Satan. Seven of the Old Testament books mention him as do all of the writers in the New Testament. Indeed, what we know about Satan is introduced near the very beginning of the Bible in Genesis 3.

Introducing Satan—the Story of the Fall (Genesis 3)

We first see Satan, the leader of the evil realm, in Genesis chapter 3. He is portrayed as a serpent but we read in Revelation 12:9 and 20:2 that this is in fact Satan.

[1]Now the serpent was more crafty than any other beast of the field that the LORD God had made.

He said to the woman, "Did God actually say, 'You shall not eat of any tree in the garden'?" [2]And the woman said to the serpent, "We may eat of the fruit of the trees in the garden, [3]but God said, 'You shall not eat of the fruit of the tree that is in the midst of the garden, neither shall you touch it, lest you die.'" [4] But the serpent said to the woman, "You will not surely die. [5]For God knows that when you eat of it your eyes will be opened, and you will be like God, knowing good and evil." [6]So when the woman saw that the tree was good for food, and that it was a delight to the eyes, and that the tree was to be desired to make one wise, she took of its fruit and ate, and she also gave some to her husband who was with her, and he ate. [7] Then the eyes of both were opened, and they knew that they were naked. And they sewed fig leaves together and made themselves loincloths.

[8]And they heard the sound of the LORD God walking in the garden in the cool of the day, and the man and his wife hid themselves from the presence of the LORD God among the trees of the garden. [9]But the LORD God called to the man and said to him, "Where are you?" [10]And he said, "I heard the sound of you in the garden, and I was afraid, because I was naked, and I hid myself." [11]He said, "Who told you that you were naked? Have you eaten of the tree of which I commanded you not to eat?" [12]The man said, "The woman whom you gave to be with me, she gave me fruit of the tree, and I ate." [13]Then the LORD God said to the woman, "What is this that you have done?" The woman said, "The serpent deceived me, and I ate."

[14]The LORD God said to the serpent, "Because you have done this, cursed are you above all livestock and above all beasts of the field; on your belly you shall go,

and dust you shall eat all the days of your life. [15]I will put enmity between you and the woman, and between your offspring and her offspring; he shall bruise your head, and you shall bruise his heel."

In the text in Genesis, we see following about Satan's character and work:

3:1—He is crafty, that is, he is brilliantly intelligent. His malignant actions are carefully planned to bring about the fullest possible harm.

3:1, 4-5—He sows doubt in the minds of God's children by twisting the truth. He knows what God has said, but he bends God's word and even contradicts it to weaken faith in God's goodness.

3:6—He tempts and deceives God's children by making evil seem good: being "good for food," a "delight to the eye," and "desired to make one wise," are all good things in and of themselves. Yet when those good things become more important than the best—obedience to God's commandments—then the abuse of that which is good is in fact evil.

3:7, 10—He desires to bring shame to his victims: nakedness was an unknown concept before the Fall. In this we also see that the "gifts" of Satan are parodies of what he promises: the Hebrew word for "wise" (cunning, 'aruum, as opposed to godly wisdom, chōkhmah) in verse 6 and "naked" ('aroom) in verse 7 are puns, words which sound and are spelled very much alike.

3:12-13—His actions lead sinners to blame others for sin rather than confession and repentance.

3:14-15—Satan is the great enemy of humankind (the Hebrew word, satan, means "adversary"). From the moment God cursed the serpent, a global war for the bodies, minds, and souls of humanity commences. This war is demonstrated in everyday life in the distinction between humans who are driven by self-love (the seed of the serpent) and those who are motivated by the love of God (the seed of the woman). That said, God gave the promise that the enmity between the serpent and the seed of the woman would ultimately result in the triumph of a particular child of Eve (Jesus Christ) over the serpent's design, despite the wounding the serpent inflicts. Genesis chapters 4 and 5 illustrate the conflict between the two races or seed-lines of man.

Who is Satan?

Satan is a person, that is, he is an intelligent being (2 Cor 11:3), with emotions (Rev 12:17) and a will (2 Tim 2:26).

Much of what we know about him is seen in his Biblical names. In the Ancient Near East, they believed one could know the character of a person by knowing his name. Thus Satan is our adversary (as we saw above, also 1 Pet 5:8); a slanderer (the meaning of the word "devil," Matt 4:1ff); the lord of flies (filth and decay, Beelzebub/l, Matt 12:24); Lucifer (the fallen bearer of light, Is 14:12); lawless (Belial, 2 Cor 6:15); the evil one (1 John 5:19); the tempter (1 Thess 3:5); the prince of this world (John 12:31); the god of this age (2 Cor 4:4); the prince of the power of the air (Eph 2:2); the accuser of the brethren (Rev 12:10); the false angel of light (2 Cor 11:14); and a serpent (Rev 12:9, which is to say the dragon of Rev 12:3).

Satan was created as an angelic being of a high rank (Eph 6:11&12; Ezek 28:12-14). Nevertheless, he is a creature—Satan is not the equal but opposite of God (as the Zoroastrians and Yezidis teach, see 1 John 4:4): he is limited (Job 1:12), finite, and *not* all-powerful—the Christian can by God's grace resist his attacks (Jam 4:7).

Satan's Fall

Ezekiel 28:11-19 is a prophetic judgment in the form of a lamentation against the King of Tyre. The consensus testimony of the church fathers was this passage is about Satan.[1] While most contemporary scholars argue that this truly is a prophecy against the

---

1. Patmore, *Adam, Satan, and the King of Tyre,* 40-67; Russell, *Satan: the Early Christian Tradition,* 131-132.

Phoenician King of Tyre using hyperbolic, apocalyptic language,[2] yet Daniel 10 & 12 speaks of Michael as the great prince of the people of Israel and of two demonic spirits who resist the Lord who are called the prince of the kingdom of Persia and the prince of Greece. It could well be argued that there is a heavenly/earthly parallel where the warfare of heaven and hell are mirrored in the political and military maneuvering of human rulers.[3] In other words, this passage in Ezekiel is likely about both the King of Tyre and Satan.

> [11]Moreover, the word of the LORD came to me: [12] "Son of man, raise a lamentation over the king of Tyre, and say to him, Thus says the Lord GOD: 'You were the signet of perfection, full of wisdom and perfect in beauty. [13]You were in Eden, the garden of God; every precious stone was your covering, sardius, topaz, and diamond, beryl, onyx, and jasper, sapphire, emerald, and carbuncle; and crafted in gold were your settings and your engravings. On the day that you were created they were prepared. [14]You were an anointed guardian cherub. I placed you; you were on the holy mountain of God; in the midst of the stones of fire you walked. [15]You were blameless in your ways from the day you were created, till unrighteousness was found in you. [16]In the abundance of your trade you were filled with violence in your midst, and you sinned; so I cast you as a profane thing from the mountain of God, and I destroyed you, O guardian cherub, from the midst of the stones of fire. [17)] Your heart was proud because of your beauty; you corrupted your wisdom for the sake of your splendor. I cast you to the ground; I exposed you before kings, to feast their eyes on you. [18]By the multitude of your iniquities, in the unrighteousness of your trade you profaned your sanctuaries; so I brought fire out from your midst; it consumed you, and I turned you to ashes on the earth in the sight of all who saw you. [19]All who know you among the peoples

2. Peterson and Cole, *Hermeneutics, Intertextuality and the Contemporary Meaning of Scripture*, 246.

3. Consider Eph 6:12.

are appalled at you; you have come to a dreadful end and shall be no more forever.'"

28:12—Satan is described as having been the signet, the seal and authority, indeed the epitome of perfection. He was full of wisdom (*chōkhmah*, godly wisdom, as opposed to cunning or guile (*'aruum*, Gen 3:1) or mere prudence (*sakhal*, Gen 3:6). His form was fully beautiful.

28:13—He had access to Eden (of course) and his beauty is comparable to all the precious gems of the Ancient Near East set in finely crafted and engraved gold.

28:14—He was the specially appointed guardian cherub, an angel of the highest rank, who had access to the presence of God.

28:15-19—He was morally upright from the day of his creation (he was created good) until sin was found in him. His evil is moral (the result of unrighteous actions) and not ontological (in his being, Satan was created good). The origin of Satan's sin (and indeed all sin) is his pride, resulting in his casting aside godly wisdom and his being made to be seen as foolish and shameful. Because of his sinful actions, he was: (1) no longer holy, he was a profane thing, (2) cast out from the presence of God, (3) cast down to the earth, and (4) consigned to a place where he is consumed by fire (see also Rev 20:10).

Many church fathers also believed that, as in Ezekiel 28, Satan is portrayed in Isaiah 14:12-14 as political leader, in this case the king of Babylon.[4] The literary form of the passage is also very similar to Ezekiel 28, that is, it is a prophetic judgment in the form of a lamentation.

---

4. So Origen, *Commentary on the Gospel of John,* 1.13, *On First Principles,* 1.5.5; Gregory of Nyssa, *Against Eunomius,* 1.22; Augustine *On Christian Doctrine,* 2.21, *City of God,* 7.15; Rufinus, *Apology, 1.34;* Tertullian, *Against Marcion,* 5.11 and 5.17. It should be admitted, however, that there were some fathers who viewed this passage as applying only to the King of Babylon. See *Manley, Isaiah through the Ages, 252.* Beginning with Calvin (*Commentary of Isaiah,* Volume I, 404), most modern scholars argue that this is only the King of Babylon. See Goldingay, *Isaiah,* 102-103.

¹² "How you are fallen from heaven, O Day Star, son of
Dawn! How you are cut down to the ground, you who
laid the nations low! ¹³You said in your heart, 'I will
ascend to heaven; above the stars of God; I will set my
throne on high; I will sit on the mount of assembly in the
far reaches of the north; ¹⁴I will ascend above the heights
of the clouds; I will make myself like the Most High.'"

14:12—Lucifer (Hebrew *heilel ben-shachar,* "bright one, son
of the dawn," "morning star, son of the dawn," or "Lucifer, son of
the dawn"), has been cast out of and fallen from the heavens. "Star"
is used elsewhere in scriptures to symbolize angels (Job 38:67 and
Rev 12:4).

14:13&14—The reasons for this fall are in his pride he deter-
mined: (1) to set himself above all the other heavenly hosts; (2) to
exercise dominion and judgment in the heavenly court; and (3) to
become like (equal to) God.

Satan's Activities

Satan works through the world, our fallen nature, and diabolic
actions (John 12:31, 5:19; Gal 5:19-21; Rom 7:18; and 1 John 2:13-
15). In Satan's interactions with Christ, we see he works via temptation (Matt 4:1-11), attack (John 8:44; Matt 16:23; and Luke 22:31),
and possession (John 13:27—Judas must have been important for
Satan himself to possess him). Satan also mentally and spiritually
blinds or otherwise hinders the understanding of non-believers (2
Cor 4:4; Luke 8:12), including the use of false religions (Rev 2:13).
In the life of the Christian, Satan tempts him/her to pride (1
Chron 21:1-8), materialism (John 2:15), immorality (1 Cor 7:5),
to lie (Acts 5:3), discouragement (1 Pet 5:6-10), and unforgive-
ness (2 Cor 2:10&11). He attempts to thwart Christian ministry
(1 Thess 2:18; Rev. 2:10). He promotes heresy (1 John 4:1-4) and
harmful emotions (anger, bitterness, and schism, Eph 4:26&27; 2
Cor 2:5-11).

APPENDIX H

Fallen Angels and Demons

The Origin of Demons

There are two theories about the origin of demons. One theory is that they are fallen angels, co-rebels with Satan. This is the traditional theory of the majority witness of the Church. The second theory is that demons are disembodied spirits, either of the dead offspring of the intermarriage of fallen angels with human women (the *nephilim* of Genesis 6)[5] or spirits deliberately created bodiless by God.[6]

The first theory maintains that the Bible only speaks clearly about two types of supernatural beings (other than God): righteous angels and fallen angels.

The second theory argues there are actually a variety of supernatural beings recorded in Scripture—seraphim (Is 6:2, 6), cherubim (Heb 9:5), archangels (Jude 9), and myriads of angels and other spirit beings (Rev 5:11), to say nothing of the diabolic hierarchy in Eph 6:12 of rulers, authorities, cosmic powers, and spiritual forces of evil. The opinion here is that demons are the spirits of the *nephilim*, the children resulting from the sexual relationships between fallen angels and human women (Gen 6:4).

To further explain, the second theory (that demons are not fallen angels but rather the *nephilim*, the children of fallen angels) is based upon this logic. While it is true that fallen angels may manifest themselves physically in our world (see below), this does not mean that this manifestation is temporary, but rather it is an intrusion of the angelic being, including an angelic body, into the physical realm. Since fallen angels have bodies, they cannot possess another body. Instead, possessions are the actions of demons, the disembodied spirits of the dead *nephilim* who attempt to possess bodies both to liberate themselves from the pains of hell and to carry out the will of the lord of their fathers, that is, Satan. Perhaps

5. Thus Enoch 15:8-12; Jubilees 10:1-17; and The Testament of the Twelve Patriarchs 1:5, all Second Temple works. Some church fathers held this view. See Louth, *Ancient Christian Commentary on Scripture,* 125-126.

6. Trachtenberg, *Jewish Magic and Superstition,* 29-30.

when the Scriptures speak of Satan possessing Judas, it actually means that a demon possessed him on Satan's behalf.

For the purpose of this lesson, we will assume the nature and actions of demons are as described in the first theory, that is, they are fallen angels. There is little practical difference when it comes to deliverance ministry.

Who are Fallen Angels?

Demons (or fallen angels) were created by God as a part of the originally righteous angelic realm (Col 1:16). However, they later fell, like Satan, as a result of moral choices. These beings are described in several places throughout the Scriptures, including Dan 10:10-20; Matt 10:1; and Eph 6:12.

The Bible clearly indicates that Satan has a host of followers—he is called the Prince of the Demons (Matt 12:24). Matthew refers to "the Devil and his angels" (Matt 25:41). Satan recruited a host of fellow rebels, apparently one third of the angelic host (Rev 12:4, where Satan is the dragon and angels are the stars, as discussed above). These followers seem to be divided into various species like the angelic hosts (see above): rulers, authorities, cosmic powers, and spiritual forces (Eph 6:12).

Like Satan, fallen angels are persons—they have intellect, emotions, and a will. Their intelligence is profound, the result of thousands of years of experience and careful observation. When all others around them had no idea who Jesus was, they did (Mark 1:14, 34; 5:6&7). They know about the judgment at the end of the age (Matt 8:28&29—which will not work well for them). They will attempt to predict the future (and must be accurate enough to make money for their human collaborators, Acts 16:16).

Demons are wicked (Eph 6:12), morally degenerate (Matt 10:1 and Jude 6&7), and evil (Luke 7:21). They are normally unseen, but like Satan (Zech 3:1; Matt 4:9&10) they can materialize (Rev 9:7; 16:13-16). They have supernatural strength as well (Mark 5:3; Acts 19:16; and Rev 9:1-11).

Activities of Demons

It is likely the case that much of the time when Satan is said to be operating, it is in fact one of his followers. They follow the example of their master in deceiving people, carrying out his diabolic plans (2 Cor. 11:15). They promote the worship of false gods—in fact they encourage people to worship them (Lev. 17:7; Deut. 32:17; Ps. 106:36-38). They are highly organized in a political/military-like structure in their attempt to thwart the Lord's plans (Eph. 6:10-12). They invent and encourage the belief in and teaching of heresy (1 Tim. 4:1), and promote all kinds of division and egoism in the church (James 3:13-16).

More spectacularly, demons can "demonize" (Greek, *daimonizoma*) people, causing all sorts of physical afflictions: epilepsy (Matt 17:15-18), blindness (Matt 12:22), severe physical handicaps (Luke 13:11), mental illnesses (Mark 5:5), suicidal behavior (Mark 9:22), and possessions (Luke 8:26-33—the demons wanted to go into the bodies of the swine). Note that sometimes God allows demonic affliction as a means of sanctification (Job 2:7-9 and 2 Cor 12:17).

Ancient Canaanite Gods as Demons.[7]

As we saw above, the false gods of Canaan, by whom Israel was led astray, are in fact demons (Deut 32:17). From the Biblical records, these wicked spirits have names and specific sin-areas in which they act. In reflecting on these demonic "gods," the reader can readily discern their current activities in our society.[8]

Baal (Ugaritic and other Semitic languages, "lord"), according to ancient Near Eastern mythology,[9] was the male fertility god who lived in the mountains. His semen would fall as rain on the ground,

7. Several references are available on these pagan deities. De Vaux, *The Early History of Israel* is very helpful.

8. Payne, *The Healing Presence*, 231-235.

9. There are several, often contradictory, traditions concerning Baal and Ashtoreth from the Ancient Near East. This reflects one of the more common.

causing it to be fertile and grow crops. Baal was not particularly faithful to his wife, Ashtoreth/Ishtar (see below) and would often sow his semen elsewhere. Baal, or perhaps spirits of Baal, can be considered as demons of *disordered male sexuality*, inducing fornication, promiscuity, adultery, sexual addictions of many kinds (including pornography), deviancy and perversion (including homosexuality, bisexuality, and sadomasochism). This perverted sexuality is primarily about the pursuit of animal appetites, that is, pleasure. A Baal spirit will seek to use this pursuit to distract men from their proper Biblical roles as protector and provider.

Ashtoreth/Ishtar/Astarte (from which we get our word Easter; she may be identical to Isis) was the fertility goddess of Canaan and Babylon (and perhaps the entire Ancient Near East). When the rains came upon the ground, it was said that the semen of Baal was impregnating her. Ashtoreth was very angry, yet patient, with Baal's infidelity, so in order to encourage him to have sex with her, her devotees would erect *asherah* poles (phallic symbols) to cause Baal to be jealous. Also, the ancient Canaanites would pair up with one another (typically not their spouses) to have sex in the fields to arouse Baal's sexual desire. Sometimes the couples would have sex in a cross-gendered manner—women dressed as men and men as women. Ashtoreth spirits are demons of *disordered female sexuality*, including many of the behaviors of Baal spirits. The primary goal of this perversion is the desire for acceptance, love, and control *at any cost*.

One particular manifestation of the Ashtoreth spirit is known in Scripture as a Jezebel spirit (Rev 2:20-23). The story of Jezebel, wife of Ahab and Queen of the northern kingdom of Israel, is well documented in 1 and 2 Kings. In these passages, three characteristics stand out: her devotion to Baal and Ashtoreth, her opposition to Yahweh and His prophets, and her efforts at controlling her husband and indeed all men around her. We see her like again in Revelation 2 when a woman called Jezebel (though this was likely not her true name but rather a description of her spirit) attempted to control the church at Thyatira through false religious devotion, heretical teaching, and sexual immorality. Pastors I interviewed and several Christian writers (such as John Paul Jackson[10]) report that those demonized by a Jezebel spirit are women, often perceived as being important in the parish, who will use every means at their disposal to control the leaders (especially pastors) of the church. They also frequently surround themselves with passive followers who have been seduced by the Jezebel spirit.[11]

Dagon, the Ugarit and later Philistine god and father of Baal, was thought at one time to be the fish god. However, archeological evidence suggests that the Philistine harbors were silted up by the time of their conflict with Israel. Instead, linguistic evidence points to the root *dag* meaning "grain." Dagon spirits would perhaps be demons of a disordered pursuit of material wealth. Consider that the devotees of Dagon sought to propitiate Yahweh with offerings of gold (1 Sam 5:1-6:16). God is not opposed to calling some of his people to material prosperity, but the pursuit of material possessions as an end in itself is idolatry and, as we have seen, idols can be demonic spirits. Dagon spirits lead to materialism, greed, jealousy, theft, exploitation, and even murder.

Molech/Milcom (of the Ammonites) and Chemosh (of the Moabites) were perhaps different names for the same god, a god of human fertility to whom children were sacrificed by burning—apparently even Solomon was guilty of worshipping this horrific god (see 1 Kings 11:3-8). Molech spirits are the demons of disordered parenting. They promote child abuse in all its forms and abortions.

10. Jackson, *Unmasking the Jezebel Spirit*. While his earlier ministry was filled with controversy, Jackson would later bring his teachings into alignment with orthodox, biblical teaching, especially under the oversight of John Wimber and the mentoring of R.T. Kendall. From a non-Pentecostal/Charismatic position more or less support Jackson's position, see Towns, *Bible Answers for Almost All your questions,* "Questions about Demons." In fairness, a scholarly disagreement of this view of the Jezebel spirit is found in Stark and Van Deventer, "The 'Jezebel spirit': A scholarly inquiry," *Verbum et Ecclesia,* 301. For what it is worth, both Dr. Stark and Dr. Van Deventer are academics at North-West University, South Africa, and not pastors.

11. If they are men, they are sometimes said to be controlled by an Ahab spirit. See Sampson, *Discerning and Defeating the Ahab Spirit.*

Appendix I

Suggested Diocesan Regulation on the Practice of Deliverance Ministry

Scope and Purpose

This regulation is the Bishop Ordinary's instructions on the practice of deliverance ministry within the _____ (name of the diocese).

1. The requirements stated in this regulation are binding on all clergy and lay ministers (licensed and/or in residence).

2. Exceptions to this regulation may only be granted by the Ordinary or his designee and must be given in writing.

Instructions

1. Deliverance ministry should only be undertaken by experienced persons authorized by the Ordinary.

   a. The ministry of exorcism may only be exercised by a minister (a priest or licensed lay minister) who is authorized for this ministry by the Ordinary.

b. Every member of a deliverance ministry team must be under a well-defined line of accountability and authority. The minister assigned by the Ordinary to supervise the deliverance ministry should be clearly identified in writing.

c. All must agree to abide by this regulation.

d. All individuals authorized for this ministry must have appropriate training and be kept up to date with current practices and teachings in the Church. This includes practices and teachings which are good and beneficial and those that are false or harmful.

e. This ministry should never be undertaken by one person ministering alone; there should always be at least one other priest or lay minister who is authorized by the Ordinary accompanying the ministry supervisor.

f. Everyone involved in performing this ministry should be covered by adequate liability insurance. The Ordinary should ensure that either the diocese or the minister's parish has an insurance policy in place to cover anyone authorized by the Ordinary to exercise this ministry.

2. It should be done in the context of prayer and sacrament.

a. Only the Ordinary can give permission for an exorcism to take place.

b. The pastor/rector of the person receiving deliverance ministry will normally be both consulted and involved.

c. Suitable resources from The Book of Common Prayer or any other sources approved by the Ordinary will normally be used.

d. The ministers involved should act in such a way that their personal conduct and Christian faith inspires trust and confidence.

e. Anyone receiving deliverance ministry must be made aware that this is a Gospel ministry of the church which calls upon the presence of the Spirit of Christ to come and bring healing and salvation in Jesus' name.

f. The sacraments, especially holy communion, are normally a key component of this ministry.

g. Language, body language, and touch should be courteous and considerate. Ministers should receive permission before touching the person receiving prayer.

h. Recipients should be made aware of what will happen in this ministry and that no one should receive ministry against his/her will.

i. All such ministry will comply with the Diocese's policies for safeguarding children, young people, and vulnerable adults, especially (but not exclusively) with regard to sexual misconduct and exploitation avoidance.

j. Any complaints about personal conduct will referred to the Ordinary for investigation.

3. It should be done in collaboration with medical and mental health professionals.

a. A multi-disciplinary approach should be taken, consulting and collaborating as necessary with doctors, psychologists and psychiatrists, and recognizing that healthcare professionals and related agencies are bound by codes of conduct.

b. In relation to counseling and psychotherapy, it should be noted that these should only be provided by suitably credentialed counselors and therapists.

4. It should be followed up by continuing pastoral care.

a. The Ordinary will assign one or more advisers for deliverance ministry who will be available for clergy and lay ministers in providing continuing pastoral care on a case-by-case basis.

b. People in receipt of such ministry must be encouraged to find a caring and supportive home within their local Christian community.

5. It should be done with the minimum of publicity.

a. The privacy and dignity of individuals and families should be respected.

b. Confidential records should be kept by those carrying out deliverance ministry to protect both those to whom they minister and those who are ministering. These records must be safeguarded in an appropriate manner, such as a locked filing cabinet or desk drawer, with limited access.

c. Any limitations to confidentiality should be explained in advance and any disclosure should be restricted to relevant information, which should be conveyed only to appropriate persons.[1]

1. Adapted from The Church of England's Pastoral Guidelines. Revised with considerable assistance from the Rev. Joel Serebrov, JD, LLM.

Bibliography

Amorth, Gabriele. *An Exorcist Tells His Story.* San Francisco: Ignatius, 1999.

———. *An Exorcist: More Stories.* San Francisco: Ignatius, 2002.

Army and Navy Commission for the Protestant Episcopal Church, The. *A Prayer Book for Soldiers and Sailors.* New York: The Church Pension Fund, 1941. http://justus.anglican.org/resources/bcp/1928/S&S_Prayers.htm.

Associated Press. "117 Hospitalized after Drinking Holy Water." http://www.cbsnews.com/ news/117-hospitalized-after-drinking-holy-water. 2010.

Baglio, Matt. *The Rite.* New York, NY: Image, 2010.

Calvin, John. *Commentary on Isaiah. Volume I.* Translated by John King. Charleston: Forgotten, 2007.

De Vaux, Roland. *The Early History of Israel.* Louisville: Westminster/Knox, 1978.

Diocese of Exeter, The. "The Church of England's Pastoral Guidelines of 1976 and revised in 2009." https://www.churchofengland.org/media/1734117/guidelines%20on%20deliverance%20ministry.pdf.

Goldingay, John. *Isaiah.* Peabody: Hendrickson, 2001.

Harper, Michael. *Spiritual Warfare.* Ann Arbor: Servant, 1984.

Hellboy. Directed by Guillermo del Toro. Los Angeles: Columbia Pictures, 2004.

Isaacs, T. Craig. *Revelations and Possession.* Kearney: Morris, 2009.

Koch, Kurt E. *Demonology Past and Present.* Grand Rapids: Kregel, 1973.

Jackson, John Paul. *Unmasking the Jezebel Spirit.* Eastbourne: Kingsway, 2001.

Maximovitch of Shanghai and San Francisco, St. John. "Selected Sermons, Part II." http://www.orthodoxphotos.com/readings/john/2/.

Lozano, Neal. *Resisting the Devil.* Huntington: Our Sunday Visitor, 2009.

———. *Unbound: A Practical Guide to Deliverance.* Grand Rapids: Chosen, 2010.

Louth, Andrew, ed. *Ancient Christian Commentary on Scripture.* Old Testament, Volume I: Genesis 1-11. Downer's Grove: InterVarsity, 2004.

MacNutt, Francis. *Deliverance from Evil Spirits*. Grand Rapids: Chosen, 2009.

Manely, Johanna. *Isaiah through the Ages*. New York: St. Vladimir's Seminary Press, 1995.

Manual for Priests, A. Fifth edition. Swedesboro: Preservation, 1996.

Martin, Malachi. *Hostage to the Devil*. New York: Reader's Digest, 1976.

Papademetriou, George C. "Exorcism in the Orthodox Church." 1996. http://www.goarch.org/ourfaith/ ourfaith7079.

Patmore, Hector G. *Adam, Satan, and the King of Tyre: the Interpretation of Ezekiel 28:11-19 in Late Antiquity*. Leiden: Brill, 2012.

Payne, Leanne. *The Healing Presence*. Grand Rapids: Baker, 1995.

———. *Restoring the Christian Soul*. Grand Rapids: Baker, 1991.

Peterson, Paul, and Ross Cole, eds. *Hermeneutics, Intertextuality, and the Contemporary Meaning of Scripture*. Cooranbong: Avondale Academic, 2013.

Richards, John. *Exorcism, Deliverance and Healing: Some Pastoral Guidelines*. Bramcote: Grove, 1976.

Russell, Jeffrey Burton. *Satan: the Early Christian Tradition*. Cornell: Cornell University Press, 1987.

Sampson, Steve. *Discerning and Defeating the Ahab Spirit*. Grand Rapids: Chosen, 2010.

Scanlan, Michael, and Michael J. Cirner. *Deliverance from Evil Spirits*. Cincinnati: St. Anthony Messenger, 1980.

Stark, S.G., and H.J.M. Van Deventer. "The 'Jezebel spirit': A scholarly inquiry." *Verbum et Ecclesia* 30.2 (2009) 1-9. www.ve.org.za/index.php/VE/article/download/301/pdf.

Steffon, Jeffrey J. *Spirit Warfare for Catholics*. Eugene: Wipf and Stock, 1994.

Strype, John. *Ecclesiastical Memorials*. Oxford: Claredon, 1822.

Toner, Patrick. "Exorcist." *The Catholic Encyclopedia*. Volume 5. New York: Robert Appleton, 1909, revised 2012. http://www.newadvent.org/cathen/05711a.htm.

Towns, Elmer. "Questions about Demons." *Bible Answers for Almost All Your Questions*. Nashville: Thomas Nelson, 2003. https://books.google.com/ books?id=dvGDi2PAZzwC&pg=PT4&source=gbs_selected_pages&cad=2#v=onepage&q&f=false.

Trachtenberg, Joshua. *Jewish Magic and Superstition: A Study in Folk Religion*. New York: Behrman's, 1939.

Unger, Merrill F. *Biblical Demonology*, revised edition. Grand Rapids: Kregel, 2011.

Made in the USA
Columbia, SC
22 August 2018